Maritime labour Conventions
and Recommendations

Maritime labour Conventions and Recommendations

International Labour Office   Geneva

ILO
Maritime labour Conventions and Recommendations third edition
Geneva, International Labour Office, 1994.

/Text/s, /ILO Convention/s, /ILO Recommendation/s, /Seafarer/s, /Persons employed on board ship/, /Maritime questions/. 01.03.7
ISBN 92-2-107111-1

ILO Cataloguing in Publication Data

CONTENTS

Safety, health and welfare

Labour inspection

Social security

Part B. International labour standards applying to all workers including seafarers

Annexes

INTRODUCTION

The International Labour Organization was created under the Treaty of Versailles in 1919 to advance the cause of social justice and thus contribute to the establishment of universal and lasting peace. This it would do by promoting the social and economic well-being of the world's people through decent living standards, satisfactory conditions of work and pay, and adequate employment opportunities. The aims and purposes of the Organization were reaffirmed in the Declaration of Philadelphia, adopted by the International Labour Conference in 1944. This Declaration lays down guiding principles such as: labour is not a commodity; freedom of expression and of association are essential to sustained progress; poverty anywhere constitutes a danger to prosperity everywhere; all human beings, irrespective of race, creed or sex, have the right to pursue both their material well-being and their spiritual development in conditions of freedom and dignity, of economic security and equal opportunity. In 1946 the ILO became the first specialized agency associated with the United Nations. The original membership of 42 nations has grown to 168 by the end of October 1993.

The main activities of the International Labour Organization are:
- the formulation of an international agenda to help improve working and living conditions, enhance employment opportunities, and promote workers' rights;
- the creation of international labour standards for national authorities to apply in putting this agenda into action;
- the implementation of a programme of international technical cooperation to help governments to carry out this agenda in practice;
- the use of training, education, research and publishing activities to help advance all these efforts.

One of the ILO's oldest and most important functions is the adoption by the tripartite International Labour Conference (in which workers' and employers' representatives have an equal voice with those of governments in formulating policies) of Conventions and Recommendations which set international labour standards. Through ratification by member States, Conventions are intended to create binding obligations to put their provisions into effect. Recommendations provide guidance on policy, legislation and practice.

Between 1919 and 1993, 174 Conventions and 181 Recommendations were adopted. Their coverage includes certain basic human rights (such as freedom of association, freedom from forced labour, and equality of opportunity in employment and occupation), labour administration, industrial relations, employment policy, working conditions, social security, occupational safety and health, protection of children, and employment of special categories such as migrant workers and seafarers.

From the very beginning in 1919 it was decided that the special questions relating to seafarers should normally be considered by special maritime sessions of the International Labour Conference devoted exclusively to them. In fact, the Second Session of the Conference, held in Genoa in 1920, was the first maritime Session, and between 1920 and 1987 a total of 36 Conventions and 26 Recommendations concerning seafarers have been adopted, which demonstrates the important part of ILO activities devoted to seafarers' questions.

The present publication contains the substance of 28 Conventions and 22 Recommendations dealing with the conditions of employment of seafarers adopted by the International Labour Conference. With the exception of Conventions Nos. 56, 91 and 109, it omits the texts of Conventions which have not received the required number of ratifications for entry into force, or are no longer open to ratifications as a result of the entry into force of a revising Convention. It also omits accompanying Recommendations on the same subjects, and Convention No. 15, which is not of current interest. It gives the substance of four ILO Conventions which apply to all workers including seafarers, but which are considered to form part of maritime minimum standards – the Freedom of Association and Protection of the Right to Organize Convention, 1948 (No. 87), the Right to Organize and Collective Bargaining Convention, 1949 (No. 98), the Medical Care and Sickness Benefits Convention, 1969 (No. 130), and the Minimum Age Convention, 1973 (No. 138). Other ILO instruments of general scope which are of importance to seafarers include the Forced Labour Convention, 1930 (No. 29), the Abolition of Forced Labour Convention, 1957 (No. 105), and the Discrimination (Employment and Occupation) Convention, 1958 (No. 111). The Conventions and Recommendations relating to fishing, inland navigation and dock work are not included.

The texts given here generally omit the formal Preamble recalling the circumstances in which the Convention or Recommendation was adopted by the Conference. They also omit a number of formal or standard Articles which appear at the end of all Conventions and are of procedural rather than substantive interest. These deal with the procedures of ratification; the time at which a Convention is to come into force (normally 12 months after the second ratification and thereafter 12 months after the subsequent ratification by the country concerned); the time when a Convention may be denounced (normally at ten-yearly intervals after its first coming into force; the submission to the International Labour Office of a report on the working of the Convention); the relation between the Convention and any revising Convention that may be adopted subsequently; application to non-metropolitan territories and the authenticity of both French and English versions of the text. Where, however, there is a point of material importance, such as a special condition for the coming into force of the Convention, the text is given.

Each member State is required by the ILO Constitution: (a) within a given limit to submit all Conventions and Recommendations adopted by the Conference to the competent national authorities for a decision as to the action to be taken on them; and (b) to report to the ILO at regular intervals on action taken to implement ratified Conventions. Government reports are evaluated by two special bodies – the Committee of Experts on the Application of Conventions and Recommendations and a tripartite Conference Committee. Member States are further required of the ILO to report on unratified Conventions or Recommendations specified by the Governing Body, showing the extent to which effect has been given, or is proposed to be given, to the provisions of such instruments. There are in addition constitutional procedures for the examination of representations made to the ILO by an industrial association of employers or of workers that a Member has failed to secure the effective observance within its jurisdiction of any Convention to which it is a party, and to investigate complaints filed by any Member which is not satisfied that any other Member is securing the effective observance of any Convention which both have ratified, or by a delegate to the International Labour Conference. The Governing Body may also initiate the complaints procedure of its own motion. A special procedure exists for the examination of allegations of infringements of trade union rights.

Part A of this volume contains the substantive provisions of the international instruments concerning seafarers adopted up to and including the 74th (Maritime) Session of the International Labour Conference in September/October 1987. Part B contains the provisions of the instruments applicable to all workers including seafarers, as referred to in Convention No. 147.

Annex I shows a list of all Conventions mentioned in chronological order; Recommendations are shown in Annex II. Annex III is a chart of ratifications by States Members as at 14 December 1993 of the maritime and other Labour Conventions listed in this publication. Annex IV shows declarations of application of Conventions to non-metropolitan territories.

It is hoped that this compilation of international labour standards for seafarers, adopted by the International Labour Organization during more than 70 years of standard-setting activities, will provide ready and useful information to all individuals, bodies and organizations interested in the employment and social aspects of maritime labour.

Geneva, December 1993

INTERNATIONAL LABOUR STANDARDS
FOR SEAFARERS

GENERAL

National Seamen's Codes Recommendation, 1920 (No. 9)

In order that, as a result of the clear and systematic codification of the national law in each country, the seamen of the world, whether engaged on ships of their own or foreign countries, may have a better comprehension of their rights and obligations, and in order that the task of establishing an International Seamen's Code may be advanced and facilitated, the International Labour Conference recommends that each Member of the International Labour Organization undertake the embodiment in a seamen's code of all its laws and regulations relating to seamen in their activities as such.

Seafarers' Engagement (Foreign Vessels) Recommendation, 1958 (No. 107)

1. Each Member should do everything in its power to discourage seafarers within its territory from joining or agreeing to join vessels registered in a foreign country unless the conditions under which such seafarers are to be engaged are generally equivalent to those applicable under collective agreements and social standards accepted by bona fide organizations of shipowners and seafarers of maritime countries where such agreements and standards are traditionally observed.

2. In particular, each Member should have regard to whether proper provision is made –

(a) for the return of a seafarer employed on a vessel registered in a foreign country who is put ashore in a foreign port for reasons for which he is not responsible to –

    (i) the port at which he was engaged; or

    (ii) a port in his own country or the country to which he belongs; or

    (iii) another port agreed upon between the seafarer concerned and the master or shipowner, with the approval of the competent authority or under other appropriate safeguards;

(b) for medical care and maintenance of a seafarer employed on a vessel registered in a foreign country who is put ashore in a foreign port in consequence of sickness or injury incurred in the service of the vessel and not due to his own wilful misconduct.

Social Conditions and Safety (Seafarers)
Recommendation, 1958 (No. 108)

Considering that labour conditions have a substantial bearing on safety of life at sea,

Considering that the problems involved have been brought into special prominence by the large volume of tonnage registered in countries not hitherto regarded as being traditionally maritime,

Considering that the Convention on the High Seas adopted by the United Nations Conference on the Law of the Sea and opened for signature on 29 April 1958 contains a set of provisions regarding –

(i) the right of every State to sail ships under its flag;

(ii) the condition relating to the nationality of the ship that "there must exist a genuine link between the State and the ship; in particular, the State must effectively exercise its jurisdiction and control in administrative, technical and social matters over ships flying its flag";

(iii) the obligation that every State shall take such measures for ships under its flag as are necessary to ensure safety at sea with regard, inter alia, to the manning of ships and labour conditions for crews taking into account the applicable international labour instruments,

Considering the provisions of the Seafarers' Engagement (Foreign Vessels) Recommendation, 1958, and

Considering the provisions of the Social Security (Seafarers) Convention, 1946;

The Conference recommends that the following provisions should be applied:

The country of registration should accept the full obligations implied by registration and exercise effective jurisdiction and control for the purpose of the safety and welfare of seafarers in its seagoing merchant ships and in particular should –

(a) make and adopt regulations designed to ensure that all ships on its register observe internationally accepted safety standards;

(b) make arrangements for a proper ship-inspection service adequate to the requirements of the tonnage on its register and ensure that all ships on its register are regularly inspected to ensure conformity with regulations issued under (a) above;

(c) establish both in its territory and abroad the requisite government controlled agencies to supervise the signing on and signing off of seafarers;

(d) ensure or satisfy itself that the conditions under which the seafarers serve are in accordance with the standards generally accepted by the traditional maritime countries;

(e) by regulations or legislation if not already otherwise provided for, ensure freedom of association for the seafarers serving on board its ships;

(f) ensure by regulations or legislation that proper repatriation for the seafarers serving on board its ships is provided in accordance with the practice followed in traditional maritime countries;

(g) ensure that proper and satisfactory arrangements are made for the examination of candidates for certificates of competency and for the issuing of such certificates.

Employment of Seafarers (Technical Developments) Recommendation, 1970 (No. 139)

I. Manpower Planning

1. Each Member which has a maritime industry should ensure the establishment of national manpower plans for that industry within the framework of its national employment policy.

2. In preparing such manpower plans account should be taken of –

(a) the conclusions drawn from periodic studies of the size of the maritime labour force, the nature and extent of employment, the distribution of the labour force by such characteristics as age and occupational group and probable future trends in these fields;

(b) studies of trends in the evolution of new techniques in the maritime industry both at home and abroad, in relation, among other things to structural changes in the industry in the form of –

   (i) changed methods of operation of ships, technically and organizationally; and

   (ii) modifications in manning scales and job contents on different types of ships;

(c) forecasts, in the light of the foregoing studies, of the probable requirements, at different dates in the future, for various categories and grades of seafarers.

3. Such manpower plans should be designed to obtain for shipowners and seafarers as well as for the community as a whole the greatest benefits from technical progress, and to protect from hardship seafarers whose employment is affected thereby.

4. (1) If they do not formulate the manpower plans themselves, representatives of shipowners' and seafarers' organizations should be consulted in connection with their formulation and subsequent adjustment, and the cooperation and participation of these organizations should be sought in the practical application of the plans.

(2) There should be regular consultation between shipowners and seafarers and their various organizations on employment problems, related to technical change.

II. RECRUITMENT AND PLACEMENT

5. Recruitment of seafarers into the maritime industry should take account of existing manpower plans and of the forecasts contained therein.

6. (1) Mobility within the maritime labour force should be facilitated by the operation of an effective employment service.

(2) Where the placement of seafarers is the concern of specialized employment offices, and where these offices are responsible for finding jobs ashore, placement in such jobs should be facilitated by close collaboration between those offices and the general public employment service.

7. (1) Having regard to natural wastage, positive steps should be taken by those responsible to avert or minimize as far as practicable the effects of any material reductions in the number of seafarers employed, by such measures as providing employment opportunities on as wide a range of ships as is reasonable and practicable, and by retraining where appropriate.

(2) The selection of seafarers to be affected by a reduction of the workforce should be made according to agreed criteria and on a basis appropriate to the special conditions of the maritime industry.

8. Up-to-date information should be made available on the nature of technical changes on board ship for the guidance of seafarers and potential seafarers.

III. TRAINING AND RETRAINING

9. Where technical changes require study of the need to train seafarers and to help them to adapt to these changes, account should be taken of the Vocational Training (Seafarers) Recommendation, 1970.

10. Where changes in functions and required skills arising from technical developments are likely to affect seafarers, basic training of those concerned, including certificated personnel, should be reviewed to take account of these changes and to ensure that seafarers are adequately trained for the functions they will be required to carry out.

11. Where the nature of technical developments so requires, consideration should be given to the possibility of retraining seafarers to enable them to take full advantage of the opportunities offered by these developments.

12. There should be consultation with shipowners' and seafarers' organizations, and between them, where technical developments are likely to lead to changes in manning scales or in certification requirements or to significant changes in the duties and functions of various categories of seafarers.

13. Changes in the duties and functions of the various categories of seafarers should be explained clearly and with adequate notice to those involved.

IV. REGULARITY OF EMPLOYMENT AND INCOME

14. (1) Consideration should be given to schemes providing regularity of employment and income for seafarers and suitable personnel to man ships.

(2) Such schemes might provide, for instance, for contracts of employment with a company or with the industry for seafarers with appropriate qualifications.

15. Consideration should also be given to arranging for seafarers, as part of the national social security system or otherwise, some form of benefits during periods of unemployment.

16. (1) Efforts should be made to meet the needs of seafarers, particularly older persons, who have special difficulty in adjusting to technical change.

(2) Amongst possible measures, consideration should be given to –

(a) retraining for other industries through government and other schemes that are available; and

(b) the provision of adequate benefits, within the framework of social security systems or other schemes, for those who are required to leave the maritime industry at an earlier age than is generally the case.

V. INTERNATIONAL COOPERATION

17. To avoid hardship to such seafarers employed in foreign ships as are likely to be affected by technical changes aboard ship, the governments and shipowners' and seafarers' organizations concerned should undertake early consultation and should cooperate with a view to –

(a) adjusting the supply of these seafarers gradually to the changing requirements of the foreign countries on whose ships they are employed; and

(b) minimizing the effects of redundancy by the joint application of relevant provisions of this Recommendation.

Continuity of Employment (Seafarers) Convention, 1976 (No. 145)
Date of entry into force: 13 June 1979

Article 1

1. This Convention applies to persons who are regularly available for work as seafarers and who depend on their work as such for their main annual income.

2. For the purpose of this Convention the term "seafarers" means persons defined as such by national law or practice or by collective agreement who are normally employed as crew members on board a seagoing ship other than –

(a) a ship of war;

(b) a ship engaged in fishing or in operations directly connected therewith or in whaling or in similar pursuits.

3. National laws or regulations shall determine when ships are to be regarded as seagoing ships for the purpose of this Convention.

4. The organizations of employers and workers concerned shall be consulted on or otherwise participate in the establishment and revision of definitions in pursuance of paragraphs 2 and 3 of this Article.

Article 2

1. In each member State which has a maritime industry it shall be national policy to encourage all concerned to provide continuous or regular employment for qualified seafarers in so far as this is practicable and, in so doing, to provide shipowners with a stable and competent workforce.

2. Every effort shall be made for seafarers to be assured minimum periods of employment, or either a minimum income or a monetary allowance, in a manner and to an extent depending on the economic and social situation of the country concerned.

Article 3

Measures to achieve the objectives set out in Article 2 of this Convention might include –

(a) contracts or agreements providing for continuous or regular employment with a shipping undertaking or an association of shipowners; or

(b) arrangements for the regularization of employment by means of the establishment and maintenance of registers or lists, by categories, of qualified seafarers.

Article 4

1. Where the continuity of employment of seafarers is assured solely by the establishment and maintenance of registers or lists, these shall include all occupational categories of seafarers in a manner determined by national law or practice or by collective agreement.

2. Seafarers on such a register or list shall have priority of engagement for seafaring.

3. Seafarers on such a register or list shall be required to be available for work in a manner to be determined by national law or practice or by collective agreement.

Article 5

1. To the extent that national laws or regulations permit, the strength of registers or lists of seafarers shall be periodically reviewed so as to achieve levels adapted to the needs of the maritime industry.

2. When a reduction in the strength of such a register or list becomes necessary, all appropriate measures shall be taken to prevent or minimize detrimental effects on seafarers, account being taken of the economic and social situation of the country concerned.

Article 6

Each member State shall ensure that appropriate safety, health, welfare and vocational training provisions apply to seafarers.

Article 7

The provisions of this Convention shall, except in so far as they are otherwise made effective by means of collective agreements, arbitration awards, or in such other manner as may be consistent with national practice, be given effect by national laws or regulations.

Continuity of Employment (Seafarers) Recommendation, 1976 (No. 154)

1. (1) Subject to the provisions of Paragraph 11, this Recommendation applies to persons who are regularly available for work as seafarers and who depend on their work as such for their main annual income.

(2) For the purpose of this Recommendation the term "seafarers" means persons defined as such by national law or practice or by collective agreement who are normally employed as crew members on board a seagoing ship other than –

(a) a ship of war;

(b) a ship engaged in fishing or in operations directly connected therewith or in whaling or in similar pursuits.

(3) National laws or regulations should determine when ships are to be regarded as seagoing ships for the purpose of this Recommendation.

(4) The organizations of employers and workers concerned should be consulted on or otherwise participate in the establishment and revision of definitions in pursuance of subparagraphs (2) and (3) of this Paragraph.

2. In so far as practicable, continuous or regular employment should be provided for all qualified seafarers.

3. (1) Except where continuous or regular employment with a particular shipowner exists, systems of allocation should be agreed upon which reduce to a minimum the necessity for attending calls for selection and allocation to a job and the time required for this purpose.

(2) In so far as practicable, these systems should preserve the right of a seafarer to select the vessel on which he is to be employed and the right of the shipowner to select the seafarer whom he is to engage.

4. Subject to conditions to be prescribed by national laws or regulations, or collective agreements, the transfer of seafarers in the regular employment of one employer to temporary work with another should be permitted when required.

5. (1) Where continuous or regular employment is not practicable, guarantees of employment and/or income should be provided in a manner and to an extent depending on the economic and social situation of the country concerned.

(2) These guarantees might include the following:

(a) employment for an agreed number of weeks or months per year, or income in lieu thereof;

(b) unemployment benefit when no work is available.

6. (1) Where the measures to obtain regular employment for seafarers provide for the establishment and maintenance of registers or lists of qualified

seafarers, criteria should be laid down for determining the seafarers to be included in such registers or lists.

(2)   Such criteria might include the following:

(a)   residence in the country concerned;

(b)   age and medical fitness;

(c)   competence and skill;

(d)   previous service at sea.

7.   When the strength of such registers or lists is reviewed by the parties concerned, account should be taken of all relevant factors, including the long-term factors such as the modernization of the maritime industry and changing trends in trade.

8.   If reduction in the overall strength of such a register or list becomes unavoidable, all necessary efforts should be made to help seafarers to find employment elsewhere through the provision of retraining facilities, as provided for in Part III of the Employment of Seafarers (Technical Developments) Recommendation, 1970, and the assistance of the public employment services.

9.   (1)   In so far as practicable, any necessary reduction in the strength of such a register or list should be made gradually and without recourse to termination of employment.   In this respect, experience with personnel planning techniques at the level of the undertaking and at industry level can be usefully applied to the maritime industry.

(2)   In determining the extent of the reduction, regard should be had to such means as –

(a)   natural wastage;

(b)   cessation of recruitment;

(c)   exclusion of men who do not derive their main means of livelihood from seafaring work;

(d)   reducing the retirement age or facilitating voluntary early retirement by the grant of pensions, supplements to state pensions, or lump-sum payments.

10.   Termination of employment should be envisaged only after due regard has been had to the means referred to in subparagraph (2) of Paragraph 9 and subject to whatever guarantees of employment may have been given.   It should be based as far as possible on agreed criteria, should be subject to adequate notice, and should be accompanied by payments such as –

(a)   unemployment insurance or other forms of social security;

(b)   severance allowance or other types of separation benefits;

(c)   such combination of benefits as may be provided for by national laws or regulations, or collective agreements.

11.   Appropriate provisions of this Recommendation should, as far as practicable and in accordance with national laws and practice and collective agreements, also be applied to persons who work as seafarers on a seasonal basis.

Merchant Shipping (Minimum Standards) Convention, 1976 (No. 147)

Date of entry into force: 28 November 1981

The General Conference of the International Labour Organization, ... having decided upon the adoption of certain proposals with regard to substandard vessels, particularly those registered under flags of convenience, ... adopts ... the following Convention:

Article 1

1.   Except as otherwise provided in this Article, this Convention applies to every seagoing ship, whether publicly or privately owned, which is engaged in the transport of cargo or passengers for the purpose of trade or is employed for any other commercial purpose.

2.   National laws or regulations shall determine when ships are to be regarded as seagoing ships for the purpose of this Convention.

3.   This Convention applies to seagoing tugs.

4.   This Convention does not apply to –

(a) ships primarily propelled by sail, whether or not they are fitted with auxiliary engines;

(b) ships engaged in fishing or in whaling or in similar pursuits;

(c) small vessels and vessels such as oil rigs and drilling platforms when not engaged in navigation, the decision as to which vessels are covered by this subparagraph to be taken by the competent authority in each country in consultation with the most representative organizations of shipowners and seafarers.

5.   Nothing in this Convention shall be deemed to extend the scope of the Conventions referred to in the Appendix to this Convention or of the provisions contained therein.

Article 2

Each Member which ratifies this Convention undertakes –

(a) to have laws or regulations laying down, for ships registered in its territory –

(i)   safety standards, including standards of competency, hours of work and manning, so as to ensure the safety of life on board ship;

(ii)   appropriate social security measures; and

(iii) shipboard conditions of employment and shipboard living arrangements, in so far as these, in the opinion of the Member, are not covered by collective agreements or laid down by competent courts in a manner equally binding on the shipowners and seafarers concerned;

and to satisfy itself that the provisions of such laws and regulations are substantially equivalent to the Conventions or Articles of Conventions referred to in the Appendix to this Convention, in so far as the Member is not otherwise bound to give effect to the Conventions in question;

(b) to exercise effective jurisdiction or control over ships which are registered in its territory in respect of –

    (i) safety standards, including standards of competency, hours of work and manning, prescribed by national laws or regulations;

    (ii) social security measures prescribed by national laws or regulations;

    (iii) shipboard conditions of employment and shipboard living arrangements prescribed by national laws or regulations, or laid down by competent courts in a manner equally binding on the shipowners and seafarers concerned;

(c) to satisfy itself that measures for the effective control of other shipboard conditions of employment and living arrangements, where it has no effective jurisdiction, are agreed between shipowners or their organizations and seafarers' organizations constituted in accordance with the substantive provisions of the Freedom of Association and Protection of the Right to Organize Convention, 1948, and the Right to Organize and Collective Bargaining Convention, 1949;

(d) to ensure that –

    (i) adequate procedures – subject to overall supervision by the competent authority, after tripartite consultation amongst that authority and the representative organizations of shipowners and seafarers where appropriate exist for the engagement of seafarers on ships registered in its territory and for the investigation of complaints arising in that connection;

    (ii) adequate procedures – subject to overall supervision by the competent authority, after tripartite consultation amongst that authority and the representative organizations of shipowners and seafarers where appropriate – exist for the investigation of any complaint made in connection with and, if possible, at the time of the engagement in its territory of seafarers of its own nationality on ships registered in a foreign country, and that such complaint as well as any complaint made in connection with and, if possible, at the time of the engagement in its territory of foreign seafarers on ships registered in a foreign country, is promptly reported by its competent authority to the competent authority of the country in which the ship is registered, with a copy to the Director-General of the International Labour Office;

(e) to ensure that seafarers employed on ships registered in its territory are properly qualified or trained for the duties for which they are engaged, due regard being had to the Vocational Training (Seafarers) Recommendation, 1970;

(f) to verify by inspection or other appropriate means that ships registered in its territory comply with applicable international labour Conventions in force which it has ratified, with the laws and regulations required by subparagraph (a) of this Article and, as may be appropriate under national law, with applicable collective agreements;

(g) to hold an official inquiry into any serious marine casualty involving ships registered in its territory, particularly those involving injury and/or loss of life, the final report of such inquiry normally to be made public.

Article 3

Any Member which has ratified this Convention shall, in so far as practicable, advise its nationals on the possible problems of signing on a ship registered in a State which has not ratified the Convention, until it is satisfied that standards equivalent to those fixed by this Convention are being applied. Measures taken by the ratifying State to this effect shall not be in contradiction with the principle of free movement of workers stipulated by the treaties to which the two States concerned may be parties.

Article 4

1.   If a Member which has ratified this Convention and in whose port a ship calls in the normal course of its business or for operational reasons receives a complaint or obtains evidence that the ship does not conform to the standards of this Convention, after it has come into force, it may prepare a report addressed to the government of the country in which the ship is registered, with a copy to the Director-General of the International Labour Office, and may take measures necessary to rectify any conditions on board which are clearly hazardous to safety or health.

2.   In taking such measures, the Member shall forthwith notify the nearest maritime, consular or diplomatic representative of the flag State and shall, if possible, have such representative present. It shall not unreasonably detain or delay the ship.

3.   For the purpose of this Article, "complaint" means information submitted by a member of the crew, a professional body, an association, a trade union or, generally, any person with an interest in the safety of the ship, including an interest in safety or health hazards to its crew.

Article 5

1.   This Convention is open to the ratification of Members which –

(a) are parties to the International Convention for the Safety of Life at Sea, 1960, or the International Convention for the Safety of Life at Sea, 1974, or any Convention subsequently revising these Conventions; and

(b) are parties to the International Convention on Load Lines, 1966, or any Convention subsequently revising that Convention; and

(c) are parties to, or have implemented the provisions of, the Regulations for Preventing Collisions at Sea of 1960, or the Convention on the International Regulations for Preventing Collisions at Sea, 1972, or any Convention subsequently revising these international instruments.

2.   This Convention is further open to the ratification of any Member which, on ratification, undertakes to fulfil the requirements to which ratification is made subject by paragraph 1 of this Article and which are not yet satisfied.

3. The formal ratifications of this Convention shall be communicated to the Director-General of the International Labour Office for registration.

Article 6

1. This Convention shall be binding only upon those Members of the Internatinal Labour Organization whose ratifications have been registered with the Director-General.

2. It shall come into force twelve months after the date on which there have been registered ratifications by at least ten Members with a total share in world shipping gross tonnage of 25 per cent.

3. Thereafter, this Convention shall come into force for any Member twelve months after the date on which its ratification has been registered.

Appendix

Minimum Age Convention, 1973 (No. 138), or Minimum Age (Sea) Convention (Revised), 1936 (No. 58), or Minimum Age (Sea) Convention, 1920 (No. 7);

Shipowners' Liability (Sick and Injured Seamen) Convention, 1936 (No. 55), or Sickness Insurance (Sea) Convention, 1936 (No. 56), or Medical Care and Sickness Benefits Convention, 1969 (No. 130);

Medical Examination (Seafarers) Convention, 1946 (No. 73);

Prevention of Accidents (Seafarers) Convention, 1970 (No. 134) (Articles 4 and 7);

Accommodation of Crews Convention (Revised), 1949 (No. 92);

Food and Catering (Ships' Crews) Convention, 1946 (No. 68) (Article 5);

Officers' Competency Certificates Convention, 1936 (No. 53) (Articles 3 and 4);[1]

Seamen's Articles of Agreement Convention, 1926 (No. 22);

Repatriation of Seamen Convention, 1926 (No. 23);

Freedom of Association and Protection of the Right to Organize Convention, 1948 (No. 87);

Right to Organize and Collective Bargaining Convention, 1949 (No. 98).

Merchant Shipping (Improvement of Standards) Recommendation, 1976 (No. 155)

1. (1) Except as otherwise provided in this Paragraph, this Recommendation applies to every seagoing ship, whether publicly or privately owned, which is engaged in the transport of cargo or passengers for the purpose of trade or is employed for any other commercial purpose.

(2) National laws or regulations should determine when ships are to be regarded as seagoing ships for the purpose of this Recommendation.

(3) This Recommendation applies to seagoing tugs.

(4) This Recommendation does not apply to –

---

[1] In cases where the established licensing system or certification structure of a State would be prejudiced by problems arising from strict adherence to the relevant standards of the Officers' Competency Certificates Convention, 1936, the principle of substantial equivalence shall be applied so that there will be no conflict with that State's established arrangements for certification.

(a) ships primarily propelled by sail, whether or not they are fitted with auxiliary engines;

(b) ships engaged in fishing or in whaling or in similar pursuits;

(c) small vessels and vessels such as oil-rigs and drilling platforms when not engaged in navigation, the decision as to which vessels are covered by this clause to be taken by the competent authority in each country in consultation with the most representative organizations of shipowners and seafarers.

(5) Nothing in this Recommendation should be deemed to extend the scope of the instruments referred to in the Appendix to the Merchant Shipping (Minimum Standards) Convention, 1976, or in the Appendix to this Recommendation.

2. Members should –

(a) ensure that the provisions of the laws and regulations provided for in Article 2, subparagraph (a), of the Merchant Shipping (Minimum Standards) Convention, 1976, and

(b) satisfy themselves that such provisions of collective agreements as deal with shipboard conditions of employment and shipboard living arrangements are at least equivalent to the Conventions or Articles of Conventions referred to in the Appendix to the Merchant Shipping (Minimum Standards) Convention, 1976.

3. In addition, steps should be taken, by stages if necessary, with a view to such laws or regulations, or as appropriate collective agreements, containing provisions at least equivalent to the provisions of the instruments referred to in the Appendix to this Recommendation.

4. (1) Pending steps for such revision of the Merchant Shipping (Minimum Standards) Convention, 1976, as may become necessary in the light of changes in the circumstances and needs of merchant shipping, cognizance should be taken in the application of that Convention, after consultation with the most representative organizations of shipowners and seafarers, of any revision of individual Conventions referred to in the Appendix thereto that has come into force.

(2) Cognizance should be taken in the application of this Recommendation, after consultation with the most representative organizations of shipowners and seafarers, of any revision of individual Conventions referred to in the Appendix thereto that has come into force and of any revision of other instruments therein referred to that has been adopted.

Appendix

Officers' Competency Certificates Convention, 1936 (No. 53);
Food and Catering (Ships' Crews) Convention, 1946 (No. 68);
Accommodation of Crews (Supplementary Provisions) Convention, 1970 (No. 133);
Prevention of Accidents (Seafarers) Convention, 1970 (No. 134);
Workers' Representatives Convention, 1971 (No. 135);
Paid Vacations (Seafarers) Convention (Revised), 1949 (No. 91); or
Seafarers' Annual Leave Convention, 1976 (No. 146);

Social Security (Seafarers) Convention, 1946 (No. 70);
Vocational Training (Seafarers) Recommendation, 1970 (No. 137); IMCO/ILO Document
for Guidance, 1975.

TRAINING AND ENTRY
INTO EMPLOYMENT

Placing of Seamen Convention, 1920 (No. 9)

Date of entry into force: 23 November 1921

Article 1

For the purpose of this Convention, the term "seamen" includes all persons, except officers, employed as members of the crew on vessels engaged in maritime navigation.

Article 2

1.   The business of finding employment for seamen shall not be carried on by any person, company, or other agency, as a commercial enterprise for pecuniary gain; nor shall any fees be charged directly or indirectly by any person, company or other agency, for finding employment for seamen on any ship.

2.   The law of each country shall provide punishment for any violation of the provisions of this Article.

Article 3

1.   Notwithstanding the provisions of Article 2, any person, company or agency, which has been carrying on the work of finding employment for seamen as a commercial enterprise for pecuniary gain, may be permitted to continue temporarily under Government licence, provided that such work is carried on under Government inspection and supervision, so as to safeguard the rights of all concerned.

2.   Each Member which ratifies this Convention agrees to take all practicable measures to abolish the practice of finding employment for seamen as a commercial enterprise for pecuniary gain as soon as possible.

Article 4

1.   Each Member which ratifies this Convention agrees that there shall be organized and maintained an efficient and adequate system of public employment

offices for finding employment for seamen without charge. Such system may be organized and maintained, either –

(a) by representative associations of shipowners and seamen jointly under the control of a central authority, or,

(b) in the absence of such joint action, by the State itself.

2. The work of all such employment offices shall be administered by persons having practical maritime experience.

3. Where such employment offices of different types exist, steps shall be taken to coordinate them on a national basis.

Article 5

Committees consisting of an equal number of representatives of shipowners and seamen shall be constituted to advise on matters concerning the carrying on of these offices. The Government in each country may make provision for further defining the powers of these committees, particularly with reference to the committees' selection of their chairmen from outside their own membership, to the degree of State supervision, and to the assistance which such committees shall have from persons interested in the welfare of seamen.

Article 6

In connection with the employment of seamen, freedom of choice of ship shall be assured to seamen and freedom of choice of crew shall be assured to shipowners.

Article 7

The necessary guarantees for protecting all parties concerned shall be included in the contract of engagement or articles of agreement, and proper facilities shall be assured to seamen for examining such contract or articles before and after signing.

Article 8

Each Member which ratifies this Convention will take steps to see that the facilities for employment of seamen provided for in this Convention shall, if necessary by means of public offices, be available for the seamen of all countries which ratify this Convention, and where the industrial conditions are generally the same.

Article 9

Each country shall decide for itself whether provisions similar to those in this Convention shall be put in force for deck officers and engineer-officers.

* * *

Articles 13 and 14: Entry into force immediately following registration of two ratifications. Thereafter, entry into force for other Members on the date on which their ratification is registered.

* * *

Article 16: Denunciation: this Convention became open to denunciation five years after it came into force.

Seamen's Articles of Agreement Convention, 1926 (No. 22)

Date of entry into force: 4 April 1928

Article 1

1.   This Convention shall apply to all seagoing vessels registered in the country of any Member ratifying this Convention and to the owners, masters and seamen of such vessels.

2.   It shall not apply to –

(a)   ships of war,

(b)   Government vessels not engaged in trade,

(c)   vessels engaged in the coasting trade,

(d)   pleasure yachts,

(e)   Indian country craft,

(f)   fishing vessels,

(g)   vessels of less than 100 tons gross registered tonnage or 300 cubic metres, nor to vessels engaged in the home trade below the tonnage limit prescribed by national law for the special regulation of this trade at the date of the passing of this Convention.

Article 2

For the purpose of this Convention the following expressions have the meanings hereby assigned to them, viz.:

(a)   the term "vessel" includes any ship or boat of any nature whatsoever, whether publicly or privately owned, ordinarily engaged in maritime navigation;

(b)   the term "seaman" includes every person employed or engaged in any capacity on board any vessel and entered on the ship's articles. It excludes masters, pilots, cadets and pupils on training ships and duly indentured apprentices, naval ratings, and other persons in the permanent service of a Government;

(c)   the term "master" includes every person having command and charge of a vessel except pilots;

(d)   the term "home trade vessel" means a vessel engaged in trade between a country and the ports of a neighbouring country within geographical limits determined by the national law.

Article 3

1.   Articles of agreement shall be signed both by the shipowner or his representative and by the seaman. Reasonable facilities to examine the articles of agreement before they are signed shall be given to the seaman and also to his adviser.

2.   The seaman shall sign the agreement under conditions which shall be prescribed by national law in order to ensure adequate supervision by the competent public authority.

3.   The foregoing provisions shall be deemed to have been fulfilled if the competent authority certifies that the provisions of the agreement have been laid before it in writing and have been confirmed both by the shipowner or his representative and by the seaman.

4.   National law shall make adequate provision to ensure that the seaman has understood the agreement.

5.   The agreement shall not contain anything which is contrary to the provisions of national law or of this Convention.

6.   National law shall prescribe such further formalities and safeguards in respect of the completion of the agreement as may be considered necessary for the protection of the interests of the shipowner and of the seaman.

Article 4

1.   Adequate measures shall be taken in accordance with national law for ensuring that the agreement shall not contain any stipulation by which the parties purport to contract in advance to depart from the ordinary rules as to jurisdiction over the agreement.

2.   This Article shall not be interpreted as excluding a reference to arbitration.

Article 5

1.   Every seaman shall be given a document containing a record of his employment on board the vessel. The form of the document, the particulars to be recorded and the manner in which such particulars are to be entered in it shall be determined by national law.

2.   The document shall not contain any statement as to the quality of the seaman's work or as to his wages.

Article 6

1.   The agreement may be made either for a definite period or for a voyage or, if permitted by national law, for an indefinite period.

2.   The agreement shall state clearly the respective rights and obligations of each of the parties.

3.   It shall in all cases contain the following particulars:

(1) the surname and other names of the seaman, the date of his birth or his age, and his birthplace;

(2) the place at which and date on which the agreement was completed;

(3) the name of the vessel or vessels on board which the seaman undertakes to serve;

(4) the number of the crew of the vessel, if required by national law;

(5) the voyage or voyages to be undertaken, if this can be determined at the time of making the agreement;

(6) the capacity in which the seaman is to be employed;

(7) if possible, the place and date at which the seaman is required to report on board for service;

(8) the scale of provisions to be supplied to the seaman, unless some alternative system is provided for by national law;

(9) the amount of his wages;

(10) the termination of the agreement and the conditions thereof, that is to say:

  (a) if the agreement has been made for a definite period, the date fixed for its expiry;

  (b) if the agreement has been made for a voyage, the port of destination and the time which has to expire after arrival before the seaman shall be discharged;

  (c) if the agreement has been made for an indefinite period, the conditions which shall entitle either party to rescind it, as well as the required period of notice for rescission; provided that such period shall not be less for the shipowner than for the seaman;

(11) the annual leave with pay granted to the seaman after one year's service with the same shipping company, if such leave is provided for by national law;

(12) any other particulars which national law may require.

Article 7

If national law provides that a list of crew shall be carried on board it shall specify that the agreement shall either be recorded in or annexed to the list of crew.

Article 8

In order that the seaman may satisfy himself as to the nature and extent of his rights and obligations, national law shall lay down the measures to be taken to enable clear information to be obtained on board as to the conditions of employment, either by posting the conditions of the agreement in a place easily accessible from the crew's quarters, or by some other appropriate means.

Article 9

1. An agreement for an indefinite period may be terminated by either party in any port where the vessel loads or unloads, provided that the notice specified in the agreement shall have been given, which shall not be less than twenty-four hours.

2. Notice shall be given in writing; national law shall provide such manner of giving notice as is best calculated to preclude any subsequent dispute between the parties on this point.

3. National law shall determine the exceptional circumstances in which notice even when duly given shall not terminate the agreement.

Article 10

An agreement entered into for a voyage, for a definite period, or for an indefinite period shall be duly terminated by –

(a) mutual consent of the parties;

(b) death of the seaman;

(c) loss or total unseaworthiness of the vessel;

(d) any other cause that may be provided in national law or in this Convention.

Article 11

National law shall determine the circumstances in which the owner or master may immediately discharge a seaman.

Article 12

National law shall also determine the circumstances in which the seaman may demand his immediate discharge.

Article 13

1. If a seaman shows to the satisfaction of the shipowner or his agent that he can obtain command of a vessel or an appointment as mate or engineer or to any other post of a higher grade than he actually holds, or that any other circumstance has arisen since his engagement which renders it essential to his interests that he should be permitted to take his discharge, he may claim his discharge, provided that without increased expense to the shipowner and to the satisfaction of the shipowner or his agent he furnishes a competent and reliable man in his place.

2. In such case, the seaman shall be entitled to his wages up to the time of his leaving his employment.

Article 14

1. Whatever the reason for the termination or rescission of the agreement an entry shall be made in the document issued to the seaman in accordance with Article 5 and in the list of crew showing that he has been discharged, and such entry shall, at the request of either party, be endorsed by the competent public authority.

2. The seaman shall at all times have the right, in addition to the record mentioned in Article 5, to obtain from the master a separate certificate as to the quality of his work or, failing that, a certificate indicating whether he has fully discharged his obligations under the agreement.

Article 15

National law shall provide the measures to ensure compliance with the terms of the present Convention,

* * *

Article 17: Entry into force immediately following registration of two ratifications. Thereafter, entry into force for other Members on the date on which their ratification is registered.

* * *

Article 21: Denunciation: this Convention became open to denunciation ten years after it first came into force.

Seafarers' Identity Documents Convention, 1958 (No. 108)

Date of entry into force: 19 February 1961

Article 1

1.　This Convention applies to every seafarer who is engaged in any capacity on board a vessel, other than a ship of war, registered in a territory for which the Convention is in force and ordinarily engaged in maritime navigation.

2.　In the event of any doubt whether any categories of persons are to be regarded as seafarers for the purpose of this Convention, the question shall be determined by the competent authority in each country after consultation with the shipowners' and seafarers' organizations concerned.

Article 2

1.　Each Member for which this Convention is in force shall issue to each of its nationals who is a seafarer on application by him a seafarer's identity document conforming with the provisions of Article 4 of this Convention: Provided that, if it is impracticable to issue such a document to special classes of its seafarers, the Member may issue instead a passport indicating that the holder is a seafarer and such passport shall have the same effect as a seafarer's identity document for the purpose of this Convention.

2.　Each Member for which this Convention is in force may issue a seafarer's identity document to any other seafarer either serving on board a vessel registered in its territory or registered at an employment office within its territory who applies for such a document.

Article 3

The seafarer's identity document shall remain in the seafarer's possession at all times.

Article 4

1.　The seafarer's identity document shall be designed in a simple manner, be made of durable material, and be so fashioned that any alterations are easily detectable.

2.　The seafarer's identity document shall contain the name and title of the issuing authority, the date and place of issue, and a statement that the document is a seafarer's identity document for the purpose of this Convention.

3.　The seafarer's identity document shall include the following particulars concerning the bearer:

(a)　full name (first and last names where applicable);

(b)　date and place of birth;

(c)　nationality;

(d)　physical characteristics;

(e)　photograph; and

(f)　signature or, if bearer is unable to sign, a thumbprint.

4. If a Member issues a seafarer's identity document to a foreign seafarer it shall not be necessary to include any statement as to his nationality, nor shall any such statement be conclusive proof of his nationality.

5. Any limit to the period of validity of a seafarer's identity document shall be clearly indicated therein.

6. Subject to the provisions of the preceding paragraphs the precise form and content of the seafarer's identity document shall be decided by the member issuing it, after consultation with the shipowners' and seafarers' organizations concerned.

7. National laws or regulations may prescribe further particulars to be included in the seafarer's identity document.

Article 5

1. Any seafarer who holds a valid seafarer's identity document issued by the competent authority of a territory for which this Convention is in force shall be readmitted to that territory.

2. The seafarer shall be so readmitted during a period of at least one year after any date of expiry indicated in the said document.

Article 6

1. Each Member shall permit the entry into a territory for which this Convention is in force of a seafarer holding a valid seafarer's identity document, when entry is requested for temporary shore leave while the ship is in port.

2. If the seafarer's identity document contains space for appropriate entries, each Member shall also permit the entry into a territory for which this Convention is in force of a seafarer holding a valid seafarer's identity document when entry is requested for the purpose of –

(a) joining his ship or transferring to another ship;

(b) passing in transit to join his ship in another country or for repatriation; or

(c) any other purpose approved by the authorities of the Member concerned.

3. Any Member may, before permitting entry into its territory for one of the purposes specified in the preceding paragraph, require satisfactory evidence, including documentary evidence from the seafarer, the owner or agent concerned, or from the appropriate consul, of a seafarer's intention and of his ability to carry out that intention. The Member may also limit the seafarer's stay to a period considered reasonable for the purpose in question.

4. Nothing in this Article shall be construed as restricting the right of a Member to prevent any particular individual from entering or remaining in its territory.

Vocational Training (Seafarers) Recommendation, 1970 (No. 137)

I. SCOPE

1. (1) This Recommendation applies to all training designed to prepare persons for work on board a publicly or privately owned seagoing ship engaged in the transport of cargo or passengers for the purpose of trade, engaged in training or engaged in scientific exploration. National laws or regulations, arbitration awards or collective agreements, as may be appropriate under national conditions, should determine when ships are to be regarded as seagoing ships.

(2) This Recommendation applies to training for the performance of the duties of persons in the deck, engine, radio or catering departments or of general purpose crews. It does not apply to fishermen.

II. OBJECTIVES OF TRAINING

2. The basic objectives of policy concerning vocational training of seafarers should be:

(a) to maintain and improve the efficiency of the shipping industry and the professional ability and potential of seafarers, with due regard to the educational needs of the latter and the economic and social interests of the country;

(b) to maintain and improve accident prevention standards on board merchant ships, both at sea and in port, in order to reduce the risk of injury;

(c) to encourage a sufficient number of suitable persons to make the merchant marine their career;

(d) to ensure that adequate induction training is given to all new recruits, ashore as far as possible, or on board ship;

(e) to provide training and retraining facilities commensurate with the current and projected manpower needs of the shipping industry for all the various categories and grades of seafarers;

(f) to provide the training facilities necessary in order that technical developments in the fields of operation, navigation and safety can be put into effect;

(g) to make training for upgrading and for promotion up to the highest ranks on board available to all seafarers with appropriate ability, and thereby to assist them to develop their efficiency, potential productivity and job satisfaction;

(h) to provide suitable practical training for the various categories and grades of seafarers;

(i) to ensure, as far as possible, the entry into employment of all trainees after completion of their courses.

III. NATIONAL PLANNING AND ADMINISTRATION

A. *Organization and coordination*

3. In planning a national education and training policy, the competent authorities in countries possessing or intending to develop a shipping industry should ensure that adequate provision is made in the general network of training

29

facilities for the training of seafarers in order to achieve the objectives set out in Paragraph 2 of this Recommendation.

4. Where national circumstances do not permit the development of facilities for the training of seafarers of all categories and grades required, collaboration with other countries, as well as with international organizations in setting up joint maritime training schemes for such seafarers as cannot be covered by national programmes should be considered.

5. (1) The training programmes of all public and private institutions engaged in the training of seafarers should be coordinated and developed in each country on the basis of approved national standards.

(2) Such programmes should be drawn up in cooperation with government departments, educational institutions and other bodies which have an intimate knowledge of the vocational training of seafarers, and should be so designed as to meet the operational requirements of the shipping industry, as established in consultation with shipowners' and seafarers' organizations.

6. Bodies which draw up such programmes should, in particular –

(a) maintain close contacts between the training institutions and all those concerned so as to keep training in line with the needs of the industry;

(b) make regular visits to the training schools with which they are concerned and be fully conversant with the programmes being carried out;

(c) ensure that information about available training opportunities is disseminated to all those concerned;

(d) cooperate in setting up and operating practical maritime training schemes;

(e) participate in establishing the general training standards provided for in Paragraph 11;

(f) participate in establishing such national certification standards as are appropriate for the various grades and categories of seafarers;

(g) promote direct cooperation between training institutions and those responsible for recruitment and employment.

7. The competent authorities and bodies, in cooperation with shipowners' and seafarers' organizations, should ensure that full information on public and private training schemes for seafarers and on conditions of entry into the shipping industry is available to those providing vocational guidance and employment counselling services, to public employment services and to vocational and technical training institutions.

8. The competent authorities and bodies should endeavour to ensure that –

(a) the facilities of shipyards, engineering workshops, manufacturers of equipment, naval installations, etc., are utilized where available and appropriate in training both officers and ratings;

(b) arrangements are made in order that, other things being equal, preference may be given in employment placement to persons who have received appropriate and recognized training.

9. (1) Training programmes should be regularly reviewed and kept up to date in the light of the developing needs of the industry.

(2) In the review of training programmes, account should be taken of the Document for Guidance, 1968 – which was prepared jointly by the International Labour Organization and the Inter-Governmental Maritime Consultative Organization and agreed by both organizations and which deals, in technical detail, with the subjects directly affecting the safety of life at sea – as well as of any subsequent amendments or additions thereto.

B. *Financing*

10. (1) Seafarers' training schemes should be systematically organized and their financing should be on a regular and adequate basis, having regard to the present and planned requirements and development of the shipping industry.

(2) Where appropriate, the government should make financial contributions to training schemes carried on by local government or private bodies. These contributions may take the form of general subsidies, grants of land, buildings or demonstration material such as boats, engines, navigational equipment and other apparatus, the provision of instructors free of charge, payment of trainees' allowances or payment of fees for trainees in day or boarding schools or on training ships.

(3) Seafarers should not, through lack of financial resources or training opportunities, be denied the possibility of reaching the highest ranks on board. Therefore, it should be possible for seafarers to earn or receive sufficient financial resources to enable them to obtain appropriate training.

(4) Training in publicly run training centres for seafarers should, where possible, be given without charge to trainees.

(5) Retraining necessitated by the introduction of technical innovations should be provided free of charge to the seafarers concerned. During the period of such retraining, seafarers should receive adequate allowances; seafarers sent to courses of such retraining by a shipowner should receive their full basic wage.

C. *Training standards*

11. Training standards should be laid down in conformity with national requirements for obtaining the various seafarers' certificates of competency. In particular, there should be laid down –

(a) the nature of medical examinations, including chest X-rays and diabetic, hearing and sight tests, required for persons entering training schemes; the standards of such examinations, particularly of the hearing and sight tests, could differ according to the departments which the persons concerned are planning to enter, but should in no case be lower than the medical standards required for entry into employment in the shipping industry;

(b) the level of general education required for admission to vocational training courses leading to certificates of competency;

(c) the subjects, such as navigation, seamanship, radio, electronics, engineering, catering and human relations, that should be included in the training curricula;

(d) the nature of any examination to be taken upon completion of training courses which are subject to examination;

(e) a procedure whereby the authorities ensure that the teaching staff of training institutions have the requisite experience and qualifications, including adequate practical and theoretical knowledge of technical and operational developments.

IV. TRAINING PROGRAMMES

12. The various training programmes should be realistically based on the work to be performed on board ship. They should be periodically reviewed and kept up to date in order to keep abreast of technical developments. They should include the following, as appropriate –

(a) training in navigation, seamanship, ship handling, signalling, cargo handling and stowage, ship maintenance, and other matters relating to the operation of merchant ships;

(b) training in the use of electronic and mechanical aids, such as radio and radar installations, radio direction-finders and compasses;

(c) theoretical and practical instruction in the use of life-saving and fire-fighting equipment, survival at sea procedures, and other aspects of the safety of life at sea;

(d) theoretical and practical instruction in the operation, maintenance and repair of main propulsion installations and auxiliary machinery, with emphasis on the types of equipment, including electronic equipment, installed in ships of the country concerned;

(e) training for the catering department as appropriate for those to be employed as stewards, cooks, waiters and galley staff, account being taken of training requirements for different categories of ships;

(f) training in accident prevention on board ship, particularly as regards safe working practices in all departments, and including personal safety as part of training in professional subjects, training in first aid, medical care and other related matters and health and physical training, especially swimming; training in medical care and particularly special training for personnel placed in charge of medical care on board should in all cases be related to the content of medical guides compiled by competent authorities and to full utilization of medical radio services;

(g) particularly in the case of trainees under 18 years of age, instruction in subjects of general educational value;

(h) instruction in elements of social and labour legislation related to merchant ship operations and to industrial relations regulations concerning seafarers, transportation economics, maritime insurance, maritime law, etc.;

(i) instruction in management techniques, including such subjects as personnel relations and work study.

13. Training programmes should be designed, inter alia, to prepare trainees for certificates of competency and should be directly related, where appropriate, to national certification standards. They should include adequate practical training and take account of any minimum age and minimum working experience laid down by the competent authorities in respect of the various grades of certificates. Account should also be taken of other nationally recognized certificates.

14. The duration of the various training programmes should be sufficient to enable trainees to assimilate the teaching given and should be determined with reference to such matters as –

(a) the level of training required for the shipboard occupation for which the course is designed;

(b) the general educational level and age required of trainees entering the course;

(c) the trainees' previous practical experience.

V. General training schemes for seafarers

15. Induction training designed to introduce trainees to the shipboard environment and safe working practices on board ship or, where appropriate and practicable, pre-sea training courses which provide adequate training for the duties regularly assigned to ratings of the deck, engine and catering departments, develop character and inculcate a sense of self-discipline and responsibility should be available for young persons with no sea experience.

16. Suitable courses or instruction should also be provided to enable young persons of appropriate ability to prepare themselves for statutory certificates or diplomas currently in effect in the merchant navy of their country in respect of both officer and rating categories.

17. Training for upgrading and promotion should, among other means, be provided by short-term courses at nautical schools and technical institutions and correspondence courses specially adapted to the needs of specific categories of officers and ratings and to the grades to which they aspire.

VI. Advanced training

18. (1) Retraining, refresher, familiarization and upgrading courses should be available as required for suitable officers and ratings to enable them to increase and widen their technical skills and knowledge, to keep abreast of technological changes, in particular in the development of automated ships, and to meet the requirements of new methods of operations on board ship.

(2) Such courses may be used for instance, to complement general courses and provide advanced specialized training opening the way to promotion, as well as to provide advanced electronics courses for appropriate personnel.

(3) Special attention should be given to the ability of masters, other officers and ratings to navigate and handle new types of ships safely.

19. Where training would be facilitated thereby, shipowners should release suitable seafarers employed on board their ships for training periods ashore, at appropriate schools, to enable them to improve their skills, learn to use new techniques and equipment and qualify for promotion. Persons in a supervisory position on board ship should take an active part in encouraging such training.

VII. TRAINING METHODS

20. The training methods adopted should be the most effective possible, having regard to the nature of the instruction, the trainees' experience, general education and age, and the demonstration equipment and financial resources available.

21. Practical training, requiring active participation of the trainees themselves should be an important part of all training programmes. It may be provided by assigning seafarers to merchant ships for periods of training at sea, to engineering workshops or shipyards or to shipping company offices.

22. Training vessels used by training institutions should provide practical instruction in navigation, seamanship, machinery operation and maintenance and other nautical subjects as well as comprehensive shipboard safety education.

23. Appropriate demonstration equipment such as simulators, engines, boat models, ship equipment, life-saving equipment, navigational aids and cargo gear should be used in training schemes. Such equipment should be selected with reference to the shipboard machinery and equipment which the trainee may be called upon to use.

24. Films and other audio-visual aids should be used, where appropriate –

(a) as a supplement to, but not a substitute for, demonstration equipment in the use of which trainees take an active part;

(b) as a primary training aid in special fields such as the teaching of languages.

25. Theoretical training and general education given as part of a training course should be related to the theoretical and practical knowledge required by seafarers;

VIII. INTERNATIONAL COOPERATION

26. Countries should cooperate in promoting the vocational training of seafarers. In some cases it may be of particular value to do so on a regional basis.

27. In so doing they might collaborate with the International Labour Organization and other international institutions, in particular the Inter-Governmental Maritime Consultative Organization, or other countries –

(a) in recruiting and training teaching staff;

(b) in setting up and improving training facilities for officers and ratings;

(c) in setting up joint training facilities with other countries where necessary;

(d) in making training facilities available to selected trainees or instructor-trainees from other countries and in sending trainees or instructor-trainees to other countries;

(e) in organizing international exchanges of personnel, information and teaching materials, as well as international seminars and working groups;

(f) in providing qualified and experienced instructors for maritime training schools in other countries.

IX. EFFECT ON EARLIER RECOMMENDATIONS

28. This Recommendation supersedes the Vocational Training (Seafarers) Recommendation, 1946.

CONDITIONS FOR ADMISSION TO EMPLOYMENT

Minimum Age (Sea) Convention, 1920 (No. 7)
Date of entry into force: 27 September 1921

Article 1

For the purpose of this Convention, the term "vessel" includes all ships and boats, of any nature whatsoever, engaged in maritime navigation, whether publicly or privately owned; it excludes ships of war.

Article 2

Children under the age of fourteen years shall not be employed on work on vessels, other than vessels upon which only members of the same family are employed.

Article 3

The provisions of Article 2 shall not apply to work done by children on school-ships or training-ships, provided that such work is approved and supervised by public authority.

Article 4

In order to facilitate the enforcement of the provisions of this Convention, every shipmaster shall be required to keep a register of all persons under the age of sixteen years employed on board his vessel, or a list of them in the articles of agreement, and of the dates of their births.

* * *

Articles 7 and 8: Entry into force immediately following registration of two ratifications. Thereafter, entry into force for other Members on the date on which their ratification is registered.

* * *

Article 10: Denunciation: the Convention became open to denunciation ten years after it first came into force.

Minimum Age (Sea) Convention (Revised), 1936 (No. 58)

Date of entry into force: 11 April 1939

Article 1

For the purpose of this Convention, the term "vessel" includes all ships and boats, of any nature whatsoever, engaged in maritime navigation, whether publicly or privately owned; it excludes ships of war.

Article 2

1.   Children under the age of fifteen years shall not be employed or work on vessels, other than vessels upon which only members of the same family are employed.

2.   Provided that national laws or regulations may provide for the issue in respect of children of not less than fourteen years of age of certificates permitting them to be employed in cases in which an educational or other appropriate authority designated by such laws or regulations is satisfied, after having due regard to the health and physical condition of the child and to the prospective as well as to the immediate benefit to the child of the employment proposed, that such employment will be beneficial to the child.

Article 3

The provisions of Article 2 shall not apply to work done by children on school-ships or training-ships, provided that such work is approved and supervised by public authority.

Article 4

In order to facilitate the enforcement of the provisions of this Convention, every shipmaster shall be required to keep a register of all persons under the age of sixteen years employed on board his vessel, or a list of them in the articles of agreement, and of the dates of their births.

Medical Examination of Young Persons (Sea) Convention, 1921 (No. 16)

Date of entry into force: 20 November 1922

Article 1

For the purpose of this Convention, the term "vessel" includes all ships and boats, of any nature whatsoever, engaged in maritime navigation, whether publicly or privately owned; it excludes ships of war.

Article 2

The employment of any child or young person under eighteen years of age on any vessel, other than vessels upon which only members for the same family are employed, shall be conditional on the production of a medical certificate attesting fitness for such work, signed by a doctor who shall be approved by the competent authority.

Article 3

The continued employment at sea of any such child or young person shall be subject to the repetition of such medical examination at intervals of not more than one year, and the production, after each such examination, of a further medical certificate attesting fitness for such work. Should a medical certificate expire in the course of a voyage, it shall remain in force until the end of the said voyage.

Article 4

In urgent cases, the competent authority may allow a young person below the age of eighteen years to embark without having undergone the examination provided for in Articles 2 and 3 of this Convention, always provided that such an examination shall be undergone at the first port at which the vessel calls.

* * *

Article 6: Entry into force immediately following registration of two ratifications. Thereafter, entry into force for other Members on the date on which their ratification is registered.

* * *

Article 10: Denunciation: the Convention became open to denunciation ten years after it first came into force.

Medical Examination (Seafarers) Convention, 1946 (No. 73)

Date of entry into force: 17 August 1955

Article 1

1. This Convention applies to every seagoing vessel, whether publicly or privately owned, which is engaged in the transport of cargo or passengers for the purpose of trade and is registered in a territory for which this Convention is in force.

2. National laws or regulations shall determine when vessels are to be regarded as seagoing.

3. This Convention does not apply to –

(a) vessels of less than 200 tons gross register tonnage;

(b) wooden vessels of primitive build such as dhows and junks;

(c) fishing vessels;

(d) estuarial craft.

Article 2

Without prejudice to the steps which should be taken to ensure that the persons mentioned below are in good health and not likely to endanger the health of other persons on board, this Convention applies to every person who is engaged in any capacity on board a vessel except –

(a) a pilot (not a member of the crew);

(b) persons employed on board by an employer other than the shipowner, except radio officers or operators in the service of a wireless telegraphy company;

(c)   travelling dockers (longshoremen) not members of the crew;

(d)   persons employed in ports who are not ordinarily employed at sea.

Article 3

1.   No person to whom this Convention applies shall be engaged for employment in a vessel to which this Convention applies unless he produces a certificate attesting to his fitness for the work for which he is to be employed at sea signed by a medical practitioner or, in the case of a certificate solely concerning his sight, by a person authorized by the competent authority to issue such a certificate.

2.   Provided that, for a period of two years from the date of the entry into force of this Convention for the territory concerned, a person may be so engaged if he produces evidence that he has been employed in a seagoing vessel to which this Convention applies for a substantial period during the previous two years.

Article 4

1.   The competent authority shall, after consultation with the shipowners' and seafarers' organizations concerned, prescribe the nature of the medical examination to be made and the particulars to be included in the medical certificate.

2.   When prescribing the nature of the examination, due regard shall be had to the age of the person to be examined and the nature of the duties to be performed.

3.   In particular, the medical certificate shall attest –

(a)   that the hearing and sight of the person and, in the case of a person to be employed in the deck department (except for certain specialist personnel, whose fitness for the work which they are to perform is not liable to be affected by defective colour vision), his colour vision, are all satisfactory; and

(b)   that he is not suffering from any disease likely to be aggravated by, or to render him unfit for, service at sea or likely to endanger the health of other persons on board.

Article 5

1.   The medical certificate shall remain in force for a period not exceeding two years from the date on which it was granted.

2.   In so far as a medical certificate relates to colour vision it shall remain in force for a period not exceeding six years from the date on which it was granted.

3.   If the period of validity of a certificate expires in the course of a voyage the certificate shall continue in force until the end of that voyage.

Article 6

1.   In urgent cases the competent authority may allow a person to be employed for a single voyage without having satisfied the requirements of the preceding articles.

2.   In such cases the terms and conditions of employment shall be the same as those of seafarers in the same category holding a medical certificate.

3.   Employment in virtue of this Article shall not be deemed on any subsequent occasion to be previous employment for the purpose of Article 3.

Article 7

The competent authority may provide for the acceptance in substitution for a medical certificate of evidence in a prescribed form that the required certificate has been given.

Article 8

Arrangements shall be made to enable a person who, after examination, has been refused a certificate to apply for a further examination by a medical referee or referees who shall be independent of any shipowner or of any organization of shipowners or seafarers.

Article 9

Any of the functions of the competent authority under this Convention may, after consultation with the organizations of shipowners and seafarers, be discharged by delegating the work, or part of it, to an organization or authority exercising similar functions in respect of seafarers generally.

* * *

Article 11

1.   This Convention shall be binding only upon those Members of the International Labour Organization whose ratifications have been registered with the Director-General.

2.   It shall come into force six months after the date on which there have been registered ratifications by seven of the following countries: United States of America, Argentine Republic, Australia, Belgium, Brazil, Canada, Chile, China, Denmark, Finland, France, United Kingdom of Great Britain and Northern Ireland, Greece, India, Ireland, Italy, Netherlands, Norway, Poland, Portugal, Sweden, Turkey and Yugoslavia, including at least four countries each of which has at least one million gross register tons of shipping. This provision is included for the purpose of facilitating and encouraging early ratification of the Convention by Member States.

3.   Thereafter, this Convention shall come into force for any Member six months after the date on which its ratification has been registered.

CERTIFICATES OF COMPETENCY

Officers' Competency Certificates Convention, 1936 (No. 53)

Date of entry into force: 29 March 1939

Article 1

1.   This Convention applies to all vessels registered in a territory for which this Convention is in force and engaged in maritime navigation with the exception of –

(a)   ships of war;

(b)   Government vessels, or vessels in the service of a public authority, which are not engaged in trade;

(c)   wooden ships of primitive build such as dhows and junks.

2.   National laws or regulations may grant exceptions or exemptions in respect of vessels of less than 200 tons gross registered tonnage.

Article 2

For the purpose of this Convention the following expressions have the meanings hereby assigned to them –

(a)   "master or skipper" means any person having command or charge of a vessel;

(b)   "navigating officer in charge of a watch" means any person, other than a pilot, who is for the time being actually in charge of the navigation or manoeuvring of a vessel;

(c)   "chief engineer" means any person permanently responsible for the mechanical propulsion of a vessel;

(d)   "engineer officer in charge of a watch" means any person who is for the time being actually in charge of the running of a vessel's engines.

Article 3

1.   No person shall be engaged to perform or shall perform on board any vessel to which this Convention applies the duties of master or skipper, naviga-

ting officer in charge of a watch, chief engineer, or engineer officer in charge of a watch, unless he holds a certificate of competency to perform such duties, issued or approved by the public authority of the territory where the vessel is registered.

2.   Exceptions to the provisions of this Article may be made only in cases of *force majeure*.

Article 4

1.   No person shall be granted a certificate of competency unless –

(a) he has reached the minimum age prescribed for the issue of the certificate in question;

(b) his professional experience has been of the minimum duration prescribed for the issue of the certificate in question; and

(c) he has passed the examinations organized and supervised by the competent authority for the purpose of testing whether he possesses the qualifications necessary for performing the duties corresponding to the certificate for which he is a candidate.

2.   National laws or regulations shall –

(a) prescribe a minimum age to have been attained by and a minimum period of professional experience to have been completed by candidates for each grade of competency certificate;

(b) provide for the organization and supervision by the competent authority of one or more examinations for the purpose of testing whether candidates for competency certificates possess the qualifications necessary for performing the duties corresponding to the certificates for which they are candidates.

3.   Any Member of the Organization may, during a period of three years from the date of its ratification, issue competency certificates to persons who have not passed the examinations organized in virtue of paragraph 2 (b) of this Article who –

(a) have in fact had sufficient practical experience of the duties corresponding to the certificate in question; and

(b) have no record of any serious technical error against them.

Article 5

1.   Each Member which ratifies this Convention shall ensure its due enforcement by an efficient system of inspection.

2.   National laws or regulations shall provide for the cases in which the authorities of a Member may detain vessels registered in its territory on account of a breach of the provisions of this Convention.

3.   Where the authorities of a Member which has ratified this Convention find a breach of its provisions on a vessel registered in the territory of another Member which has also ratified the Convention, the said authorities shall communicate with the consul of the Member in the territory of which the vessel is registered.

Article 6

1.   National laws or regulations shall prescribe penalties or disciplinary measures for cases in which the provisions of this Convention are not respected.

2.   In particular, such penalties or disciplinary measures shall be prescribed for cases in which –

(a)   a shipowner, shipowner's agent, master or skipper has engaged a person not certificated as required by this Convention;

(b)   a master or skipper has allowed any of the duties defined in Article 2 of this Convention to be performed by a person not holding the corresponding or a superior certificate;

(c)   a person has obtained by fraud or forged documents an engagement to perform any of the duties defined in the said Article 2 without holding the requisite certificate.

Certification of Ships' Cooks Convention, 1946 (No. 69)

Date of entry into force: 22 April 1953

Article 1

1.   This Convention applies to seagoing vessels, whether publicly or privately owned, which are engaged in the transport of cargo or passengers for the purpose of trade and registered in a territory for which this Convention is in force.

2.   National laws or regulations or, in the absence of such laws or regulations, collective agreements between employers and workers shall determine the vessels or classes of vessels which are to be regarded as seagoing vessels for the purpose of this Convention.

Article 2

For the purpose of this Convention the term "ship's cook" means the person directly responsible for the preparation of meals for the crew of the ship.

Article 3

1.   No person shall be engaged as ship's cook on board any vessel to which this Convention applies unless he holds a certificate of qualification as ship's cook granted in accordance with the provisions of the following articles.

2.   Provided that the competent authority may grant exemptions from the provisions of this Article if in its opinion there is an inadequate supply of certificated ships' cooks.

Article 4

1.   The competent authority shall make arrangements for the holding of examinations and for the granting of certificates of qualification.

2.   No person shall be granted a certificate of qualification unless –

(a)   he has reached a minimum age to be prescribed by the competent authority;

(b) he has served at sea for a minimum period to be prescribed by the competent authority; and

(c) he has passed an examination to be prescribed by the competent authority.

3.   The prescribed examination shall provide a practical test of the candidate's ability to prepare meals; it shall also include a test of his knowledge of food values, the drawing up of varied and properly balanced menus, and the handling and storage of food on board ship.

4.   The prescribed examination may be conducted and certificates granted either directly by the competent authority or, subject to its control, by an approved school for the training of cooks or other approved body.

Article 5

Article 3 of this Convention shall apply after the expiration of a period not exceeding three years from the date of entry into force of the Convention for the territory where the vessel is registered: Provided that, in the case of a seaman who has had a satisfactory record of two years' service as cook before the expiration of the aforesaid period, national laws or regulations may provide for the acceptance of a certificate of such service as equivalent to a certificate of qualification.

Article 6

The competent authority may provide for the recognition of certificates of qualification issued in other territories.

Article 7

The formal ratifications of this Convention shall be communicated to the Director-General of the International Labour Office for registration.

Article 8

1.   This Convention shall be binding only upon those Members of the International Labour Organization whose ratifications have been registered with the Director-General.

2.   It shall come into force six months after the date on which there have been registered ratifications by nine of the following countries: United States of America, Argentine Republic, Australia, Belgium, Brazil, Canada, Chile, China, Denmark, Finland,, France, United Kingdom of Great Britain and Northern Ireland, Greece, India, Ireland, Italy, Netherlands, Norway, Poland, Portugal, Sweden, Turkey and Yugoslavia, including at least five countries each of which has at least one million gross register tons of shipping. This provision is included for the purpose of facilitating and encouraging early ratification of the Convention by Member States.

3.   Thereafter, this Convention shall come into force for any Member six months after the date on which its ratification has been registered.

Certification of Able Seamen Convention, 1946 (No. 74)

Date of entry into force: 14 July 1951

Article 1

No person shall be engaged on any vessel as an able seaman unless he is a person who by national laws or regulations is deemed to be competent to perform any duty which may be required of a member of the crew serving in the deck department (other than an officer of leading or specialist rating) and unless he holds a certificate of provisions of the following articles.

Article 2

1. The competent authority shall make arrangements for the holding of examinations and for the granting of certificates of qualification.

2. No person shall be granted a certificate of qualification unless –

(a) he has reached a minimum age to be prescribed by the competent authority;

(b) he has served at sea in the deck department for a minimum period to be prescribed by the competent authority; and

(c) he has passed an examination of proficiency to be prescribed by the competent authority.

3. The prescribed minimum age shall not be less than eighteen years.

4. The prescribed minimum period of service at sea shall not be less than thirty-six months: Provided that the competent authority may –

(a) permit persons with a period of actual service at sea of not less than twenty-four months who have successfully passed through a course of training in an approved training school to reckon the time spent in such training, or part thereof, as sea service; and

(b) permit persons trained in approved seagoing training ships who have served eighteen months in such ships to be certificated as able seamen upon leaving in good standing.

5. The prescribed examination shall provide a practical test of the candidate's knowledge of seamanship and of his ability to carry out effectively all the duties that may be required of an able seaman, including those of a lifeboatman; it shall be such as to qualify a successful candidate to hold the special lifeboatman's certificate provided for in Article 22 of the International Convention for the Safety of Life at Sea, 1929, or in the corresponding provision of any subsequent Convention revising or replacing that Convention for the time being in force for the territory concerned.

Article 3

A certificate of qualification may be granted to any person who, at the time of the entry into force of this Convention for the territory concerned, is performing the full duties of an able seaman or leading deck rating or has performed such duties.

Article 4

The competent authority may provide for the recognition of certificates of qualification issued in other territories.

GENERAL CONDITIONS OF EMPLOYMENT

Wages, Hours of Work and Manning (Sea)
Convention (Revised), 1958 (No. 109)

Date of entry into force: Not in force by 14 December 1993

PART I. GENERAL PROVISIONS

Article 1

Nothing in this Convention shall be deemed to prejudice any provision concerning wages, hours of work on board ship, or manning, by law, award, custom or agreement between shipowners and seafarers, which ensures the seafarers conditions more favourable than those provided for by this Convention.

Article 2

1. This Convention applies to every vessel, whether publicly or privately owned, which is –

(a) mechanically propelled;

(b) registered in a territory for which the Convention is in force;

(c) engaged in the transport of cargo or passengers for the purpose of trade; and

(d) engaged in a voyage by sea.

2. This Convention does not apply to –

(a) vessels of less than 500 gross register tons;

(b) wooden vessels of primitive build such as dhows and junks;

(c) vessels engaged in fishing or in operations directly connected therewith;

(d) estuarial craft.

Article 3

This Convention applies to every person who is engaged in any capacity on board a vessel except –

(a) a master;

(b) a pilot not a member of the crew;

(c) a doctor;

(d) nursing staff engaged exclusively on nursing duties and hospital staff;

(e) a chaplain;

(f) persons engaged exclusively on educational duties;

(g) a musician;

(h) persons whose duties are connected solely with the cargo on board;

(i) persons working exclusively on their own account or remunerated exclusively by a share of profits or earnings;

(j) persons not remunerated for their services or remunerated only by a nominal salary or wage;

(k) persons, excluding those in the service of a wireless telegraphy company, who are employed on board by an employer other than the shipowner;

(1) travelling dockers (longshoremen) not members of the crew;

(m) persons employed in whale-catching, floating factory or transport vessels or otherwise for the purpose of whaling or similar operations under conditions regulated by legislation or by the provisions of a special collective whaling or similar agreement determining hours of work and other conditions of service concluded by an organization of seafarers;

(n) persons who are not members of the crew (whether working on or off articles) but are employed while the vessel is in port on repairing, cleaning, loading or unloading the vessel or similar work or on port relief, maintenance, watch or caretaking duties.

Article 4

In this Convention –

(a) the term "officer" means a person other than a master who is described in the ship's articles as an officer or who is serving in a capacity which by law, collective agreement or custom is recognized as that of an officer;

(b) the term "rating" means a member of the crew other than a master or officer and includes a certificated seaman;

(c) the term "able seaman" means any person who by national laws or regulations, or in the absence of such laws or regulations by collective agreement is deemed to be competent to perform any duty which may be required of a rating serving in the deck department other than the duties of a leading or specialist rating;

(d) the term "basic pay or wages" means the remuneration of an officer or rating in cash exclusive of the cost of food, overtime, premiums or any other allowances either in cash or in kind.

Article 5

1.   Each Member ratifying this Convention may, by a declaration appended to its ratification, exclude from its ratification Part II of the Convention.

2.   Subject to the terms of any such declaration, the provisions of Part II of the Convention shall have the same effect as the other provisions of the Convention.

3.   Any Member which makes such a declaration shall also supply information showing the basic pay or wages for a calendar month of service of an able seaman employed in a vessel to which the Convention applies.

4.   Any Member which makes such a declaration may subsequently by a new declaration, notify the Director-General that it accepts Part II; as from the date of the registration of such notification by the Director-General the provisions of Part II shall be applicable to the Member in question.

5.   While a declaration made under paragraph 1 of this Article remains in force in respect of Part II, the Member may declare its willingness to accept Part II as having the force of a Recommendation.

PART II. WAGES

Article 6

1.   The basic pay or wages for a calendar month of service of an able seaman employed in a vessel to which this Convention applies shall not be less than sixteen pounds in currency of the United Kingdom of Great Britain and Northern Ireland or sixty-four dollars in currency of the United States of America or the equivalent thereof in other currency.

2.   In respect of any change in the par value of the pound or the dollar notified to the International Monetary Fund since 29 June 1946, or in the event of any further such change being notified subsequent to the adoption of this Convention –

(a)   the minimum basic wage prescribed in paragraph 1 of this Article in terms of the currency in respect of which such notification has been made shall be adjusted so as to maintain equivalence with the other currency;

(b)   the adjustment shall be notified by the Director-General of the International Labour Office to the Members of the International Labour Organization; and

(c)   the minimum basic wage so adjusted shall be binding upon Members which have ratified the Convention in the same manner as the wage prescribed in paragraph 1 of this Article, and shall take effect for each such Member not later than the beginning of the second calendar month following that in which the Director-General communicates the change to Members.

Article 7

1.   In the case of ships in which are employed such groups of ratings as necessitate the employment of larger groups of ratings than would otherwise be

employed the minimum basic pay or wages of an able seaman shall be an amount fixed as the adjusted equivalent of the minimum basic pay or wages stipulated in the preceding Article.

2.   The adjusted equivalent shall be fixed in accordance with the principle of equal pay for equal work and due allowance shall be made for –

(a) the extra number of ratings of such groups who are employed; and

(b) any increase or decrease in cost to the shipowner consequent on the employment of such groups of ratings.

3.   The adjusted equivalent shall be determined by collective agreement between the organizations of shipowners and seafarers concerned or, failing such agreement and subject to both countries concerned having ratified the Convention, by the competent authority of the territory of the group of seafarers concerned.

Article 8

If meals are not provided free of charge, the minimum basic pay or wages shall be increased by an amount to be determined by collective agreement between the organizations of shipowners and seafarers concerned or, failing such agreement, by the competent authority.

Article 9

1.   The rate to be used for determining the equivalent in other currency of the minimum basic pay or wages prescribed in Article 6 shall be the ratio between the par value of that currency and the par value of the pound of the United Kingdom of Great Britain and Northern Ireland or of the dollar of the United States of America.

2.   In the case of the currency of a Member of the International Labour Organization which is a Member of the International Monetary Fund, the par value shall be that currently in effect under the Articles of Agreement of the International Monetary Fund.

3.   In the case of the currency of a Member of the International Labour Organization which is not a Member of the International Monetary Fund, the par value shall be the official rate of exchange, in terms of gold or of the dollar of the United States of America of the weight and fineness in effect on 1 July 1944, currently in effect for payments and transfers for current international transactions.

4.   In the case of any currency which cannot be dealt with under the provisions of either of the two preceding paragraphs –

(a) the rate to be adopted for the purpose of this Article shall be determined by the Member of the International Labour Organization concerned;

(b) the Member concerned shall notify its decision to the Director-General of the International Labour Office, who shall forthwith inform the other Members which have ratified this Convention;

(c) within a period of six months from the date on which the information is communicated by the Director-General, any other Member which has ratified the Convention may inform the Director-General of the International Labour Office that it objects to the decision, and the Director-General shall thereupon inform the Member concerned and the other Members which have ratified the Convention and shall report the matter to the Committee provided for in Article 22;

(d) the foregoing provisions shall apply in the event of any change in the decision of the Member concerned.

5. A change in basic pay or wages as a result of a change in the rate for determining the equivalent in other currency shall take effect not later than the beginning of the second calendar month following that in which the change in the relative par values of the currencies concerned becomes effective.

Article 10

Each Member shall take the necessary measures –

(a) to ensure, by way of a system of supervision and sanctions, that remuneration is paid at not less than the rate required by this Convention; and

(b) to ensure that any person who has been paid at a rate less than that required by this Convention is enabled to recover, by an inexpensive and expeditious judicial or other procedure, the amount by which he has been underpaid.

PART III. HOURS OF WORK ON BOARD SHIP

Article 11

This Part of this Convention does not apply to –

(a) a chief officer or chief engineer;

(b) a purser;

(c) any other officer in charge of a department who does not keep watch;

(d) a person employed in the clerical or catering department of a vessel who is –

  (i) serving in a superior grade as defined by a collective agreement between the organizations of shipowners and seafarers concerned; or

  (ii) working chiefly on his own account; or

  (iii) remunerated solely on a commission basis or chiefly by a share of profits or earnings.

Article 12

In this Part of this Convention –

(a) the term "near trade ship" means a vessel exclusively engaged in voyages up – on which it does not proceed farther from the country from which it trades than the nearby ports of neighbouring countries within geographical limits which –

  (i) are clearly specified by national laws, regulations or by collective agreement between organizations of shipowners and seafarers;

  (ii) are uniform in respect of the application of all the provisions of this Part of the Convention;

(iii) have been notified by the Member when registering its ratification by a declaration annexed thereto; and

(iv) have been fixed after consultation with the other Members concerned;

(b) the term "distant trade ship" means a vessel other than a near trade ship;

(c) the term "passenger ship" means a vessel licensed to carry more than twelve passengers;

(d) the term "hours of work" means time during which a person is required by the orders of a superior to do work on account of the vessel or the owner.

Article 13

1. This Article applies to officers and ratings employed in the deck, engine-room and radio departments of near trade ships.

2. The normal hours of work of an officer or rating shall not exceed –

(a) when the vessel is at sea, twenty-four hours in any period of two consecutive days;

(b) when the vessel is in port –

   (i) on the weekly day of rest, such time not exceeding two hours as is necessary for ordinary routine and sanitary duties;

   (ii) on other days, eight hours except where a collective agreement provides for less on any day;

(c) one hundred and twelve hours in a period of two consecutive weeks.

3. Time worked in excess of the limits prescribed in subparagraphs (a) and (b) of paragraph 2 shall be regarded as overtime for which the officer or rating concerned shall be entitled to compensation in accordance with the provisions of Article 18 of this Convention.

4. When the total number of hours worked in a period of two consecutive weeks, excluding hours regarded as overtime, exceeds one hundred and twelve, the officer or rating concerned shall be compensated by time off in port or otherwise as may be determined by collective agreement between the organizations of shipowners and seafarers concerned.

5. National laws or regulations or collective agreements shall determine when a ship is to be regarded as being at sea and when it is to be regarded as being in port for the purposes of this Article.

Article 14

1. This Article applies to officers and ratings employed in the deck, engine-room and radio departments of distant trade ships.

2. When the vessel is at sea and on days of sailing and arrival, the normal hours of work of an officer or rating shall not exceed eight hours in any one day.

3. When the vessel is in port, the normal hours of work of an officer or rating shall not exceed –

(a) on the weekly day of rest, such time not exceeding two hours as is necessary for ordinary routine and sanitary duties;

(b) on other days, eight hours except where a collective agreement provides for less on any day.

4.   Time worked in excess of the daily limits prescribed in the preceding paragraphs shall be regarded as overtime for which the officer or rating shall be entitled to compensation in accordance with the provisions of Article 18 of this Convention.

5.   When the total number of hours worked in a period of one week, excluding hours regarded as overtime, exceeds forty-eight, the officer or rating shall be compensated by time off in port or otherwise as may be determined by collective agreement between the organizations of shipowners and seafarers concerned.

6.   National laws or regulations or collective agreements shall determine when a ship is to be regarded as being at sea and when it is to be regarded as being in port for the purposes of this Article.

Article 15

1.   This Article applies to persons employed in the catering department of a vessel.

2.   In the case of a passenger ship, normal hours of work shall not exceed –

(a) when the vessel is at sea and on days of sailing and arrival, ten hours in any consecutive period of fourteen hours;

(b) when the vessel is in port –

   (i)   when passengers are on board, ten hours in any period of fourteen hours;

   (ii) in other cases –

      on the day preceding the weekly day of rest, five hours,

      on the weekly day of rest, five hours for persons engaged in messing duties and such time not exceeding two hours as is necessary for ordinary routine and sanitary duties in the case of other persons,

      on any other day, eight hours.

3.   In the case of a vessel not a passenger ship, normal hours of work shall not exceed –

(a) when the vessel is at sea and on days of sailing and arrival, nine hours in any period of thirteen hours;

(b) when the vessel is in port –

    on the weekly day of rest, five hours;

    on the day preceding the weekly day of rest, six hours;

    on any other days, eight hours in any period of twelve hours.

4.   When the total number of hours worked in a period of two consecutive weeks exceeds one hundred and twelve the person concerned shall be compen-

sated by time off in port or otherwise as may be determined by collective agreement between the organizations of shipowners and seafarers concerned.

5.   National laws or regulations or collective agreements between the organizations of shipowners and seafarers concerned may make special arrangements for the regulation of the hours of work of night watchmen.

Article 16

1.   This Article applies to officers and ratings employed in near and distant trade ships.

2.   Time off in port should be the subject of negotiations between the organizations of shipowners and seafarers concerned on the basis that officers and ratings should receive the maximum time off in port that is practicable and that such time off should not count as leave.

Article 17

1.   The competent authority may exempt from the application of this Part of this Convention officers not already excluded therefrom by virtue of Article 11, subject to the following conditions:

(a)   the officers must be entitled in virtue of a collective agreement to conditions of employment which the competent authority certifies constitute full compensation for the non-application of this Part of the Convention;

(b)   the collective agreement must have been originally concluded before 30 June 1946 and the agreement or a renewal thereof must be still in force.

2.   A Member having recourse to the provisions of paragraph 1 shall supply to the Director-General of the International Labour Office full particulars of any such collective agreement and the Director-General shall lay a summary of the information received by him before the Committee referred to in Article 22.

3.   The said Committee shall consider whether the collective agreements reported to it provide for conditions of employment which constitute full compensation for the non-application of this Part of this Convention. Each Member ratifying the Convention undertakes to give consideration to any observations or suggestions made by the Committee concerning such agreements and further undertakes to bring any such observations or suggestions to the notice of the organizations of shipowners and officers who are parties to such agreements.

Article 18

1.   The rate or rates of compensation for overtime shall be prescribed by national laws or regulations or be fixed by collective agreement, but in no case shall the hourly rate of payment for overtime be less than one-and-a-quarter times the basic pay or wages per hour.

2.   Collective agreements may provide for compensation by equivalent time off duty and off the vessel in lieu of cash payment or for any other method of compensation.

Article 19

1.   The consistent working of overtime shall be avoided whenever possible.

2.   Time spent in the following work shall not be included in normal hours of work or be regarded as overtime for the purpose of this Part of this Convention –

(a) work that the master deems to be necessary and urgent for the safety of the vessel, cargo or persons on board;

(b) work required by the master for the purpose of giving assistance to other vessels or persons in distress;

(c) musters, fire, lifeboat and similar drills of the kind prescribed by the International Convention for the Safety of Life at Sea for the time being in force;

(d) extra work for the purposes of customs or quarantine or other health formalities;

(e) normal and necessary work by officers for the determination of the position of the ship and for making meteorological observations;

(f) extra time required for the normal relieving of watches.

3.   Nothing in this Convention shall be deemed to impair the right and duty of the master of a vessel to require, or the duty of an officer or rating to perform, any work deemed by the master to be necessary for the safe and efficient operation of the vessel.

Article 20

1.   No person under the age of sixteen years shall work at night.

2.   For the purpose of this Article, "night" means a period of at least nine consecutive hours between times before and after midnight to be prescribed by national laws or regulations or collective agreements.

PART IV. MANNING

Article 21

1.   Every vessel to which this Convention applies shall be sufficiently and efficiently manned for the purposes of –

(a) ensuring the safety of life at sea;

(b) giving effect to the provisions of Part III of this Convention; and

(c) preventing excessive strain upon the crew and avoiding or minimizing as far as practicable the working of overtime.

2.   Each Member undertakes to maintain, or to satisfy itself that there is maintained, efficient machinery for the investigation and settlement of any complaint or dispute concerning the manning of a vessel.

3.   Representatives of the organizations of shipowners and seafarers shall participate, with or without other persons or authorities, in the operation of such machinery.

PART V. APPLICATION OF THE CONVENTION

Article 22

1. Effect may be given to this Convention by (a) laws or regulations; (b) collective agreements between shipowners and seafarers (except as regards paragraph 2 of Article 21); or (c) a combination of laws or regulations and collective agreements between shipowners and seafarers. Except as may be otherwise provided herein, the provisions of this Convention shall be made applicable to every vessel registered in the territory of the ratifying Member and to every person engaged on any such vessel.

2. Where effect has been given to any provision of this Convention by a collective agreement in pursuance of paragraph 1 of this Article, then notwithstanding anything contained in Article 10 of this Convention the Member shall not be required to take any measures in pursuance of Article 10 of this Convention in respect of the provisions of the Convention to which effect has been so given by collective agreement.

3. Each Member ratifying this Convention shall supply to the Director-General of the International Labour Office information on the measures by which the Convention is applied, including particulars of any collective agreements in force which give effect to any of its provisions.

4. Each Member ratifying this Convention undertakes to take part, by means of a tripartite delegation, in any Committee representative of governments and shipowners' and seafarers' organizations, and including, in an advisory capacity, representatives of the Joint Maritime Commission of the International Labour Office, which may be set up for the purpose of examining the measures taken to give effect to the Convention.

5. The Director-General shall lay before the said Committee a summary of the information received by him under paragraph 3 above.

6. The Committee shall consider whether the collective agreements reported to it give full effect to the provisions of the Convention. Each Member ratifying the Convention undertakes to give consideration to any observations or suggestions concerning the application of the Convention made by the Committee, and further undertakes to bring to the notice of the organizations of shipowners and of seafarers who are parties to any of the collective agreements mentioned in paragraph 1 any observations or suggestions of the aforesaid Committee concerning the degree to which such agreements give effect to the provisions of the Convention.

Article 23

1. Each Member which ratifies this Convention shall be responsible for the application of its provisions to vessels registered in its territory and shall, except where effect is given to the Convention by collective agreements, maintain in force laws or regulations which –

(a) determine the respective responsibilities of the shipowner and the master for ensuring compliance therewith;

(b) prescribe adequate penalties for any violation thereof;

(c) provide for adequate public supervision of compliance with Part IV of the Convention;

(d) require the keeping of the records of hours worked necessary for the purposes of Part III of the Convention and of the compensation granted in respect of overtime and of excess hours of work;

(e) ensure to seafarers the same remedies for recovering payments due to them in respect of compensation for overtime and for excess hours of work as they have for recovering other arrears of pay.

2. The organizations of shipowners and seafarers concerned shall, so far as is reasonable and practicable, be consulted in the framing of all laws or regulations for giving effect to the provisions of this Convention.

Article 24

For the purpose of giving mutual assistance in the enforcement of this Convention, every Member which ratifies the Convention undertakes to require the competent authority in every port in its territory to inform the consular or other appropriate authority of any other such Member of any case in which it comes to the notice of such authority that the requirements of the Convention are not being complied with in a vessel registered in the territory of that other Member.

PART VI. FINAL PROVISIONS

Article 25

1. This Convention revises the Wages, Hours of Work and Manning (Sea) Conventions, 1946 and 1949.

2. For the purpose of Article 28 of the Hours of Work and Manning (Sea) Convention, 1936, this Convention shall also be regarded as a Convention revising that Convention.

* * *

Article 27

1. This Convention shall be binding only upon those Members of the International Labour Organization whose ratifications have been registered with the Director-General.

2. It shall first come into force six months after the date at which the following conditions have been fulfilled –

(a) the ratifications of nine of the following Members have been registered: Argentina, Australia, Belgium, Brazil, Canada, Chile, China, Denmark, Finland, France, Federal Republic of Germany, Greece, India, Ireland, Italy, Japan, Netherlands, Norway, Poland, Portugal, Spain, Sweden, Turkey, Union of Soviet Socialist Republics, United Kingdom of Great Britain and Northern Ireland, United States of America, Yugoslavia;

(b) at least five of the Members whose ratifications have been registered have at the date of registration each not less than 1 million gross register tons of shipping;

(c) the aggregate tonnage of shipping possessed at the time of registration by the Members whose ratifications have been registered is not less than 15 million gross register tons.

3. The provisions of the preceding paragraph are included for the purpose of facilitating and encouraging early ratification of the Convention by member States.

4. After the Convention has first come into force, it shall come into force for any Member six months after the date on which its ratification has been registered.

Article 28: Denunciation: after the Convention has been in force for five years, it will be open to denunciation at five-yearly intervals.

Wages, Hours of Work and Manning (Sea) Recommendation, 1958 (No. 109)

SCOPE

1. This Recommendation applies to seafarers, other than masters, employed in mechanically propelled seagoing ships engaged in trade but excluding estuarial craft, fishing vessels and primitive vessels.

WAGES

2. The basic pay or wages for a calendar month of service of an able seaman employed in a vessel to which this Recommendation applies should not be less than the equivalent of twenty-five pounds in currency of the United Kingdom of Great Britain and Northern Ireland or seventy dollars in currency of the United States of America,[1] whichever of these amounts may from time to time be the greater: Provided that, in determining the minimum pay or wages in the case of ships in which are employed such groups of ratings as necessitate the employment of larger groups of ratings than would otherwise be employed, and having regard to the principle of equal pay for equal work, special factors may be taken into account, such as the extra numbers employed and any differences in crew costs incurred by the shipowner consequent upon the employment of such ratings.

3. Except where effect is given to the preceding paragraph by collective agreement between bona fide organizations representing shipowners and seafarers, each Member should –

(a) ensure, by way of a system of supervision and sanctions, that remuneration is paid at not less than the rate required by the preceding paragraph; and

---

[1] In a resolution adopted at its 26th Session (October 1991), the ILO Joint Maritime Commission recommended updating the amounts to £208 sterling and US$356 respectively, as of 25 October 1991.

(b) ensure that any person who has been paid at a rate less than that required by the preceding paragraph is enabled to recover, by an inexpensive and expeditious judicial or other procedure, the amount by which he has been underpaid.

HOURS OF WORK

4. At sea and in port the normal hours of work should be eight per day for all departments. As regards hours in port on the weekly day of rest and the day preceding it, special provisions should be laid down by national laws or regulations or collective agreements.

5. When the vessel is at sea on the weekly day of rest seafarers should be compensated as may be determined by collective agreements or national laws or regulations.

6. In the case of smaller vessels and of vessels engaged on short voyages, collective agreements or national laws or regulations may provide for the averaging of the eight-hour day.

7. The rate or rates of compensation for overtime should be prescribed by national laws or regulations or be fixed by collective agreement, but in no case should the hourly rate of payment for overtime be less than one-and-a-quarter times the basic pay or wages per hour. National laws or regulations or collective agreements may provide for compensation by equivalent time off duty and off the vessel in lieu of cash payment or for any other method of compensation.

8. National laws or regulations or collective agreements should determine the duties the time spent on which should not be included in normal hours of work or be regarded as overtime for the purpose of this Recommendation.

9. Collective agreements may for special reasons provide for special arrangements as adequate compensation in lieu of direct payment of overtime.

MANNING

10. A sufficient number of officers and men should be engaged so as to ensure the avoidance of excessive overtime and to satisfy the dictates of safety of life at sea.

11. Each Member should maintain, or satisfy itself that there is maintained, efficient machinery for the investigation and settlement of any complaint or dispute concerning the manning of a vessel.

12. Representatives of the bona fide organizations of shipowners and seafarers should participate, with or without other persons or authorities, in the operation of such machinery.

GENERAL

13. Nothing in this Recommendation shall be deemed to prejudice any provision concerning wages, hours of work on board ship or manning, by law, award, custom or agreement between shipowners and seafarers, which ensures the seafarers conditions more favourable than those provided for by this Recommendation.

Paid Vacations (Seafarers) Convention (Revised), 1949 (No. 91)

Date of entry into force: 14 September 1967

Article 1

1.   This Convention applies to every seagoing mechanically propelled vessel, whether publicly or privately owned, engaged in the transport of cargo or passengers for the purpose of trade and registered in a territory for which this Convention is in force.

2.   National laws or regulations shall determine when vessels are to be regarded as seagoing vessels.

3.   This Convention does not apply to –

(a)   wooden vessels of primitive build such as dhows and junks;

(b)   vessels engaged in fishing or in operations directly connected therewith or in sealing or similar pursuits;

(c)   estuarial craft.

4.   National laws or regulations or collective agreements may provide for the exemption from the provisions of this Convention of vessels of less than 200 gross register tons.

Article 2

1.   This Convention applies to every person who is engaged in any capacity on board a vessel except –

(a)   a pilot not a member of the crew;

(b)   a doctor not a member of the crew;

(c)   nursing staff engaged exclusively on nursing duties and hospital staff not members of the crew;

(d)   persons working exclusively on their own account or remunerated exclusively by a share of profits or earnings;

(e)   persons not remunerated for their services or remunerated only by a nominal salary or wage;

(f)   persons employed on board by an employer other than the shipowner, except radio officers or operators in the service of a wireless telegraphy company;

(g)   travelling dockers (longshoremen) not members of the crew;

(h)   persons employed in whale-catching vessels, in floating factories, or otherwise for the purpose of whaling or similar operations under conditions regulated by the provisions of a special collective whaling or similar agreement determining the rates of pay, hours of work and other conditions of service concluded by an organization of seafarers;

(i)   persons employed in port who are not ordinarily employed at sea.

2.   The competent authority may, after consultation with the organizations of shipowners and seafarers concerned, exempt from the application of the Convention masters, chief navigating officers and chief engineers who by virtue

of national laws or regulations or collective agreements enjoy conditions of service which are not less favourable in respect of annual leave than those required by the Convention.

Article 3

1.   Every person to whom this Convention applies shall be entitled after twelve months of continuous service to an annual vacation holiday with pay, the duration of which shall be –

(a) in the case of masters, officers and radio officers or operators, not less than eighteen working days for each year of service;

(b) in the case of other members of the crew, not less than twelve working days for each year of service.

2.   A person with not less than six months of continuous service shall on leaving such service be entitled in respect of each complete month of service to one and a half working days' leave in the case of a master, officer, or radio officer or operator, and one working day's leave in the case of another member of the crew.

3.   A person who is discharged through no fault of his own before he has completed six months of continuous service shall on leaving such service be entitled in respect of each complete month of service to one and a half working days' leave in the case of a master, officer, or radio officer or operator, and one working day's leave in the case of another member of the crew.

4.   For the purpose of calculating when a vacation holiday is due –

(a) service off articles shall be included in the reckoning of continuous service;

(b) short interruptions of service not due to the act or fault of the employee and not exceeding a total of six weeks in any twelve months shall not be deemed to break the continuity of the periods of service which precede and follow them;

(c) continuity of service shall not be deemed to be interrupted by any change in the management or ownership of the vessel or vessels in which the person concerned has served.

5.   The following shall not be included in the annual vacation holiday with pay –

(a) public and customary holidays;

(b) interruptions of service due to sickness or injury.

6.   National laws or regulations or collective agreements may provide for the division into parts of an annual vacation holiday due in virtue of this Convention or for the accumulation of such a vacation holiday due in respect of one year with a subsequent vacation holiday.

7.   National laws or regulations or collective agreements may, in very exceptional circumstances when the service so requires, provide for the substitution for an annual vacation holiday due in virtue of this Convention of a cash payment at least equivalent to the remuneration provided for in Article 5.

Article 4

1. When an annual vacation holiday is due it shall be given by mutual agreement at the first opportunity as the requirements of the service allow.

2. No person may be required without his consent to take the annual vacation holiday due to him at a port other than a port in the territory of engagement or a port in his home territory. Subject to this requirement, the vacation holiday shall be given at a port permitted by national laws or regulations or collective agreement.

Article 5

1. Every person taking a vacation holiday in virtue of Article 3 of this Convention shall receive in respect of the full period of the vacation holiday his usual remuneration.

2. The usual remuneration payable in virtue of the preceding paragraph, which may include a suitable subsistence allowance, shall be calculated in a manner which shall be prescribed by national laws or regulations or fixed by collective agreement.

Article 6

Subject to the provisions of paragraph 7 of Article 3 any agreement to relinquish the right to an annual vacation holiday with pay, or to forgo such a vacation holiday, shall be void.

Article 7

A person who leaves or is discharged from the service of his employer before he has taken a vacation holiday due to him shall receive in respect of every day of vacation holiday due to him in virtue of this Convention the remuneration provided for in Article 5.

Article 8

Each Member which ratifies this Convention shall ensure the effective application of its provisions.

Article 9

Nothing in this Convention shall affect any law, award, custom or agreement between shipowners and seamen which ensures more favourable conditions than those provided by this Convention.

Article 10

1. Effect may be given to this Convention by (a) laws or regulations; (b) collective agreements between shipowners and seafarers; or (c) a combination of laws or regulations and collective agreements between shipowners and seafarers. Except as may be otherwise provided herein, the provisions of this Convention shall be made applicable to every vessel registered in the territory of the ratifying Member and to every person engaged on any such vessel.

2. Where effect has been given to any provision of this Convention by a collective agreement in pursuance of paragraph 1 of this Article, then, notwith-

standing anything contained in Article 8 of this Convention, the Member in whose territory the agreement is in force shall not be required to take any measures in pursuance of Article 8 in respect of the provisions of the Convention to which effect has been given by collective agreement.

3. Each Member ratifying this Convention shall supply to the Director-General of the International Labour Office information on the measures by which the Convention is applied, including particulars of any collective agreements which give effect to any of its provisions and are in force at the date when the Member ratifies the Convention.

4. Each Member ratifying this Convention undertakes to take part, by means of a tripartite delegation, in any committee representative of Governments and shipowners' and seafarers' organizations, and including in an advisory capacity representatives of the Joint Maritime Commission of the International Labour Office, which may be set up for the purpose of examining the measures taken to give effect to the Convention.

5. The Director-General will lay before the said Committee a summary of the information received by him under paragraph 3 above.

6. The Committee shall consider whether the collective agreements reported to it give full effect to the provisions of this Convention. Each Member ratifying the Convention undertakes to give consideration to any observations or suggestions concerning the application of the Convention made by the Committee and further undertakes to bring to the notice of the organizations of employers and of workers who are parties to any of the collective agreements mentioned in paragraph 1 any observations or suggestions of the aforesaid Committee concerning, the degree to which such agreements give effect to the provisions of the Convention.

Article 11

For the purpose of Article 17 of the Holidays with Pay (Sea) Convention, 1936, the present Convention shall be regarded as a Convention revising that Convention.

* * *

Articles 13 and 18: Entry into force and revision: the Convention contains special conditions, but it is closed to further ratification since the entry into force of Convention No. 146, which revises it.

Seafarers' Annual Leave with Pay Convention, 1976 (No. 146)

Date of entry into force: 13 June 1979

Article 1

The provisions of this Convention, in so far as they are not otherwise made effective by means of collective agreements, arbitration awards, court decisions, statutory wage-fixing machinery, or in such other manner consistent with national practice as may be appropriate under national conditions, shall be given effect by national laws or regulations.

Article 2

1. This Convention applies to all persons who are employed as seafarers.

2. For the purpose of this Convention, the term "seafarer" means a person who is employed in any capacity on board a seagoing ship registered in a territory for which the Convention is in force, other than –

(a) a ship of war;

(b) a ship engaged in fishing or in operations directly connected therewith or in whaling or similar pursuits.

3. National laws or regulations shall determine, after consultation with the organizations of shipowners and seafarers concerned, where such exist, which ships are to be regarded as seagoing ships for the purpose of this Convention.

4. Each Member which ratifies this Convention may, after consultation with the organizations of employers and workers concerned, where such exist, extend its application, with the modifications rendered necessary by the conditions of the industry, to the persons excluded from the definition of seafarers by paragraph 2, subparagraph (b), of this Article, or to certain categories thereof.

5. Each Member which extends the application of this Convention in pursuance of paragraph 4 of this Article at the time of ratifying it shall specify in a declaration appended to its ratification the categories to which the application is extended and the modifications, if any, rendered necessary.

6. Each Member which has ratified this Convention may further subsequently notify the Director-General of the International Labour Office, by a declaration, that it extends the application of the Convention to categories beyond those, if any, specified at the time of ratification.

7. In so far as necessary, measures may be taken by the competent authority or through the appropriate machinery in a country, after consultation with the organizations of shipowners and seafarers concerned, where such exist, to exclude from the application of this Convention limited categories of persons employed on board seagoing ships.

8. Each Member which ratifies this Convention shall list, in the first report on the application of the Convention submitted under article 22 of the Constitution of the International Labour Organization, any categories which may have been excluded in pursuance of paragraphs 3 and 7 of this Article, giving the reasons for such exclusion, and shall state in subsequent reports the position of its law and practice in respect of the categories excluded and the extent to which effect has been given or is proposed to be given to the Convention in respect of such categories.

Article 3

1. Every seafarer to whom this Convention applies shall be entitled to annual leave with pay of a specified minimum length.

2. Each Member which ratifies this Convention shall specify the length of the annual leave in a declaration appended to its ratification.

3.   The leave shall in no case be less than 30 calendar days for one year of service.

4.   Each Member which has ratified this Convention may subsequently notify the Director-General of the International Labour Office, by a further declaration, that it specifies annual leave longer than that specified at the time of ratification.

Article 4

1.   A seafarer whose length of service in any year is less than that required for the full entitlement prescribed in the preceding Article shall be entitled in respect of that year to annual leave with pay proportionate to his length of service during that year.

2.   The expression "year" in this Convention shall mean the calendar year or any other period of the same length.

Article 5

1.   The manner in which the length of service is calculated for the purpose of leave entitlement shall be determined by the competent authority or through the appropriate machinery in each country.

2.   Under conditions to be determined by the competent authority or through the appropriate machinery in each country, service off articles shall be counted as part of the period of service.

3.   Under conditions to be determined by the competent authority or through the appropriate machinery in each country, absence from work to attend an approved maritime vocational training course or for such reasons beyond the control of the seafarer concerned as illness, injury or maternity shall be counted as part of the period of service.

Article 6

The following shall not be counted as part of the minimum annual leave with pay prescribed in Article 3, paragraph 3, of this Convention:

(a)   public and customary holidays recognized as such in the country of the flag, whether or not they fall during the annual leave with pay;

(b)   periods of incapacity for work resulting from illness, injury or maternity, under conditions to be determined by the competent authority or through the appropriate machinery in each country;

(c)   temporary shore leave granted to a seafarer while on articles;

(d)   compensatory leave of any kind, under conditions to be determined by the competent authority or through the appropriate machinery in each country.

Article 7

1.   Every seafarer taking the annual leave envisaged in this Convention shall receive in respect of the full period of that leave at least his normal remuneration (including the cash equivalent of any part of that remuneration which is paid in

kind), calculated in a manner to be determined by the competent authority or through the appropriate machinery in each country.

2.   The amounts due in pursuance of paragraph 1 of this Article shall be paid to the seafarer concerned in advance of the leave, unless otherwise provided by national laws or regulations or in an agreement applicable to him and the employer.

3.   A seafarer who leaves or is discharged from the service of his employer before he has taken annual leave due to him shall receive in respect of such leave due to him the remuneration provided for in paragraph 1 of this Article.

Article 8

1.   The division of the annual leave with pay into parts, or the accumulation of such annual leave due in respect of one year together with a subsequent period of leave, may be authorized by the competent authority or through the appropriate machinery in each country.

2.   Subject to paragraph 1 of this Article and unless otherwise provided in an agreement applicable to the employer and the seafarer concerned, the annual leave with pay prescribed by this Convention shall consist of an uninterrupted period.

Article 9

In exceptional cases, provision may be made by the competent authority or through the appropriate machinery in each country for the substitution for annual leave due in virtue of this Convention of a cash payment at least equivalent to the remuneration provided for in Article 7.

Article 10

1.   The time at which the leave is to be taken shall, unless it is fixed by regulation, collective agreement, arbitration award or other means consistent with national practice, be determined by the employer after consultation and, as far as possible, in agreement with the seafarer concerned or his representatives.

2.   No seafarer shall be required without his consent to take annual leave due to him at a place other than that where he was engaged or recruited, whichever is nearer his home, except that under the provisions of a collective agreement or of national laws or regulations.

3.   If a seafarer is required to take his annual leave from a place other than that permitted by paragraph 2 of this Article, he shall be entitled to free transportation to the place where he was engaged or recruited, whichever is nearer his home, and subsistence and other costs directly involved in his return there shall be for the account of the employer; the travel time involved shall not be deducted from the annual leave with pay due to the seafarer.

Article 11

Any agreement to relinquish the right to the minimum annual leave with pay prescribed in Article 3, paragraph 3, or – except as provided, exceptionally, in pursuance of Article 9 of this Convention – to forgo such leave, shall be null and void.

Article 12

A seafarer taking annual leave shall be recalled only in cases of extreme emergency, with due notice.

Article 13

Effective measures appropriate to the manner in which effect is given to the provisions of this Convention shall be taken to ensure the proper application and enforcement of regulations or provisions concerning annual leave with pay, by means of adequate inspection or otherwise.

Article 14

This Convention revises the Paid Vacations (Seafarers) Convention (Revised), 1949 (No. 91).

Repatriation of Seamen Convention, 1926 (No. 23)

Date of entry into force: 16 April 1928

Article 1

1.   This Convention shall apply to all seagoing vessels registered in the country of any Member ratifying this Convention, and to the owners, masters and seamen of such vessels.

2.   It shall not apply to –

(a) ships of war,

(b) Government vessels not engaged in trade,

(c) vessels engaged in the coasting trade,

(d) pleasure yachts,

(e) Indian country craft,

(f) fishing vessels,

(g) vessels of less than 100 tons gross registered tonnage or 300 cubic metres, nor to vessels engaged in the home trade below the tonnage limit prescribed by national law for the special regulation of this trade at the date of the passing of this Convention.

Article 2

For the purpose of this Convention the following expressions have the meanings hereby assigned to them, viz.:

(a) the term "vessel" includes any ship or boat of any nature whatsoever, whether publicly or privately owned, ordinarily engaged in maritime navigation;

(b) the term "seaman" includes every person employed or engaged in any capacity on board any vessel and entered on the ship's articles. It excludes masters, pilots, cadets and pupils on training ships and duly indentured apprentices, naval ratings, and other persons in the permanent service of a Government;

(c) the term "master" includes every person having command and charge of a vessel except pilots;

(d) the term "home trade vessel" means a vessel engaged in trade between a country and the ports of a neighbouring country within geographical limits determined by the national law.

Article 3

1. Any seaman who is landed during the term of his engagement or on its expiration shall be entitled to be taken back to his own country, or to the port at which he was engaged, or to the port at which the voyage commenced, as shall be determined by national law, which shall contain the provisions necessary for dealing with the matter, including provisions to determine who shall bear the charge of repatriation.

2. A seaman shall be deemed to have been duly repatriated if he has been provided with suitable employment on board a vessel proceeding to one of the destinations prescribed in accordance with the foregoing paragraph.

3. A seaman shall be deemed to have been repatriated if he is landed in the country to which he belongs, or at the port at which he was engaged, or at a neighbouring port, or at the port at which the voyage commenced.

4. The conditions under which a foreign seaman engaged in a country other than his own has the right to be repatriated shall be as provided by national law or, in the absence of such legal provisions, in the articles of agreement. The provisions of the preceding paragraphs shall, however, apply to a seaman engaged in a port of his own country.

Article 4

The expenses of repatriation shall not be a charge on the seaman if he has been left behind by reason of –

(a) injury sustained in the service of the vessel, or

(b) shipwreck, or

(c) illness not due to his own wilful act or default, or

(d) discharge for any cause for which he cannot be held responsible.

Article 5

1. The expenses of repatriation shall include the transportation charges, the accommodation and the food of the seaman during the journey. They shall also include the maintenance of the seaman up to the time fixed for his departure.

2. When a seaman is repatriated as member of a crew, he shall be entitled to remuneration for work done during the voyage.

Article 6

The public authority of the country in which the vessel is registered shall be responsible for supervising the repatriation of any member of the crew in cases where this Convention applies, whatever may be his nationality, and where necessary for giving him his expenses in advance.

* * *

Article 8: Entry into force immediately following registration of two ratifications. Thereafter, entry into force for other Members on the date on which their ratification is registered.

* * *

Article 12: Denunciation: this Convention became open to denunciation ten years after it first came into force.

Repatriation (Ship Masters and Apprentices) Recommendation, 1926 (No. 27)

The Conference recommends that the national Governments shall take steps to provide for the repatriation of masters and duly indentured apprentices, who are not covered by the terms of the Convention on the repatriation of seamen adopted by the General Conference at its Ninth Session.

Repatriation of Seafarers Convention (Revised), 1987 (No. 166)

Date of entry into force: 6 July 1991

PART I. SCOPE AND DEFINITIONS

Article 1

1.   This Convention applies to every seagoing ship whether publicly or privately owned which is registered in the territory of any Member for which the Convention is in force and which is ordinarily engaged in commercial maritime navigation and to the owners and seafarers of such ships.

2.   To the extent it deems practicable, after consultation with the representative organizations of fishing vessel owners and fishermen, the competent authority shall apply the provisions of this Convention to commercial maritime fishing.

3.   In the event of doubt as to whether or not any ships are to be regarded as engaged in commercial maritime navigation or commercial maritime fishing for the purpose of this Convention, the question shall be determined by the competent authority after consultation with the organizations of shipowners, seafarers and fishermen concerned.

4.   For the purpose of this Convention the term "seafarer" means any person who is employed in any capacity on board a seagoing ship to which this Convention applies.

PART II. ENTITLEMENTS

Article 2

1.   A seafarer shall be entitled to repatriation in the following circumstances:

(a)   if an engagement for a specific period or for a specific voyage expires abroad;

(b) upon the expiry of the period of notice given in accordance with the provisions of the articles of agreement or the seafarer's contract of employment;

(c) in the event of illness or injury or other medical condition which requires his or her repatriation when found medically fit to travel;

(d) in the event of shipwreck;

(e) in the event of the shipowner not being able to continue to fulfil his or her legal or contractual obligations as an employer of the seafarer by reason of bankruptcy, sale of ship, change of ship's registration or any other similar reason;

(f) in the event of a ship being bound for a war zone, as defined by national laws or regulations or collective agreements, to which the seafarer does not consent to go;

(g) in the event of termination or interruption of employment in accordance with an industrial award or collective agreement, or termination of employment for any other similar reason.

2.   National laws or regulations or collective agreements shall prescribe the maximum duration of service periods on board following which a seafarer is entitled to repatriation; such periods shall be less than 12 months. In determining the maximum periods, account shall be taken of factors affecting the seafarers' working environment. Each Member shall seek, wherever possible, to reduce these periods in the light of technological changes and developments and may be guided by any recommendations made on the matter by the Joint Maritime Commission.

PART III. DESTINATION

Article 3

1.   Each Member for which this Convention is in force shall prescribe by national laws or regulations the destinations to which seafarers may be repatriated.

2.   The destinations so prescribed shall include the place at which the seafarer agreed to enter into the engagement, the place stipulated by collective agreement, the seafarer's country of residence or such other place as may be mutually agreed at the time of engagement. The seafarer shall have the right to choose from among the prescribed destinations the place to which he or she is to be repatriated.

PART IV. ARRANGEMENTS FOR REPATRIATION

Article 4

1.   It shall be the responsibility of the shipowner to arrange for repatriation by appropriate and expeditious means. The normal mode of transport shall be by air.

2.   The cost of repatriation shall be borne by the shipowner.

3.   Where repatriation has taken place as a result of a seafarer being found, in accordance with national laws or regulations or collective agreements, to be in

serious default of his or her employment obligations, nothing in this Convention shall prejudice the right of recovery from the seafarer of repatriation costs or part thereof in accordance with national laws or regulations or collective agreements.

4.   The cost to be borne by the shipowner shall include:

(a) passage to the destination selected for repatriation in accordance with Article 3 above;

(b) accommodation and food from the moment the seafarer leaves the ship until he or she reaches the repatriation destination;

(c) pay and allowances from the moment he or she leaves the ship until he or she reaches the repatriation destination, if provided for by national laws or regulations or collective agreements;

(d) transportation of 30 kg of the seafarer's personal luggage to the repatriation destination;

(e) medical treatment when necessary until the seafarer is medically fit to travel to the repatriation destination.

5.   The shipowner shall not require the seafarer to make an advance payment towards the cost of repatriation at the beginning of his or her employment, nor shall the shipowner recover the cost of repatriation from the seafarer's wages or other entitlements except as provided for in paragraph 3 above.

6.   National laws or regulations shall not prejudice any right of the shipowner to recover the cost of repatriation of seafarers not employed by the shipowner from their employer.

Article 5

If a shipowner fails to make arrangements for or to meet the cost of repatriation of a seafarer who is entitled to be repatriated –

(a) the competent authority of the Member in whose territory the ship is registered shall arrange for and meet the cost of the repatriation of the seafarer concerned, if it fails to do so, the State from which the seafarer is to be repatriated or the State of which he or she is a national may arrange for his or her repatriation and recover the cost from the Member in whose territory the ship is registered;

(b) costs incurred in repatriating the seafarer shall be recoverable from the shipowner by the Member in whose territory the ship is registered;

(c) the expenses of repatriation shall in no case be a charge upon the seafarer, except as provided for in paragraph 3 of Article 4 above.

PART V. OTHER ARRANGEMENTS

Article 6

Seafarers who are to be repatriated shall be able to obtain their passport and other identity documents for the purpose of repatriation.

Article 7

Time spent awaiting repatriation and repatriation travel time shall not be deducted from paid leave accrued to the seafarer.

Article 8

A seafarer shall be deemed to have been duly repatriated when he or she is landed at a destination prescribed pursuant to Article 3 above, or when the seafarer does not claim his or her entitlement to repatriation within a reasonable period of time to be defined by national laws or regulations or collective agreements.

Article 9

The provisions of this Convention in so far as they are not otherwise made effective by means of collective agreements or in such other manner as may be appropriate under national conditions shall be given effect by national laws or regulations.

Article 10

Each Member shall facilitate the repatriation of seafarers serving on ships which call at its ports or pass through its territorial or internal waters, as well as their replacement on board.

Article 11

The competent authority of each Member shall ensure by means of adequate supervision that the owners of ships registered in its territory comply with the provisions of the Convention, and shall provide relevant information to the International Labour Office.

Article 12

The text of this Convention shall be available in an appropriate language to the crew members of every ship which is registered in the territory of any Member for which it is in force.

Article 13

This Convention revises the Repatriation of Seamen Convention, 1926.

Repatriation of Seafarers Recommendation, 1987 (No. 174)

Whenever a seafarer is entitled to be repatriated pursuant to the provisions of the Repatriation of Seafarers Convention (Revised), 1987, but both the shipowner and the Member in whose territory the ship is registered fail to meet their obligations under the Convention to arrange for and meet the cost of repatriation, the State from which the seafarer is to be repatriated or the State of which he or she is a national should arrange for his or her repatriation, and recover the cost from the Member in whose territory the ship is registered in accordance with Article 5 (a) of the Convention.

Protection of Young Seafarers Recommendation, 1976 (No. 153)

I. METHODS OF IMPLEMENTATION

1.   Effect may be given to this Recommendation through national laws or regulations, collective agreements, works rules, arbitration awards or court decisions, or in such other manner as may be appropriate under national conditions.

II. DEFINITION AND SCOPE

2.   (1) For the purpose of this Recommendation, the term "young seafarer" includes all young persons under 18 years of age employed in any capacity on board a seagoing ship other than –

(a)   a ship of war; and

(b)   a ship engaged in fishing or in operations directly connected therewith or in whaling or similar pursuits.

(2)   National laws or regulations should determine, after consultation with the organizations of employers and workers concerned, when ships are to be regarded as seagoing ships for the purpose of this Recommendation.

(3)   This Recommendation does not apply to young persons in school or training vessels or pursuing an educational programme carried out in accordance with conditions approved by the competent authority after consultation with the organizations of employers and workers concerned.

III. OBJECTIVES

3.   In each country in which ships in which young seafarers are employed are registered, provision should be made for –

(a)   the effective protection of such seafarers, including the safeguarding of their health, morals and safety, and the promotion of their general welfare;

(b)   vocational guidance, education and vocational training of such seafarers, in their interest as well as that of the efficiency of shipboard operations, in the interest of safety of life and of property at sea and in that of the creation of opportunities for the advancement of young seafarers within the seagoing profession.

IV. HOURS OF PERMITTED DUTY AND REST PERIODS

4.   (1)   At sea and in port the provisions set out in the following clauses should apply:

(a)   the normal working hours of young seafarers should not exceed eight hours per day and forty hours per week and the consistent working of overtime should be avoided whenever possible;

(b)   while sufficient time should be allowed for all meals, young seafarers should be assured of a break of at least one hour for the main meal of the day;

(c)   no young seafarer should work at night; for the purpose of this clause "night" means a period of at least nine consecutive hours between times before and after midnight to be prescribed by national laws or regulations or by collective agreements;

(d) young seafarers should be allowed a 15-minute rest period as soon as possible following each two hours of continuous work.

(2) Exceptionally, the provisions of subparagraph (1) of this Paragraph need not be applied –

(a) if they are impracticable for young seafarers in the deck, engine-room and catering departments assigned to watchkeeping duties or working on a rostered shift-work system;

(b) if the effective training of young seafarers in accordance with established programmes and schedules would be impaired; or

(c) in cases of operational necessity.

Such exceptions should be recorded, with reasons, and signed by the captain.

5.   The provisions of paragraph 4 of this Recommendation do not exempt young seafarers from their general obligation to work under the master's direction during any emergency involving –

(a)   the safety of the crew, the passengers, the vessel or its cargo;

(b)   the safety of other vessels or of lives and cargoes on board such vessels.

V. REPATRIATION

6.   (1)   If, after a young seafarer has served in a vessel for at least four months during his first foreign-going voyage, it becomes apparent that he is unsuited to life at sea, he should be given the opportunity of being repatriated at no expense to himself from the first suitable port of call in which there are consular services of the country either of the flag of the ship or of the nationality of the young seafarer. Notification of any such repatriation, with the reasons therefor, should be given to the authority which issued the papers enabling the young seafarer to take up seagoing employment.

(2)   After six months' service without leave in a foreign-going vessel which has not returned to the young seafarer's country of residence in that time, and will not so return in the subsequent three months of the voyage, a young seafarer should be entitled to be repatriated at no expense to himself to the place of original engagement in his country of residence for the purpose of taking any leave earned during the voyage.

VI. SAFETY IN WORK AND HEALTH EDUCATION

7.   Regulations concerning safety and health of young seafarers should be adopted.

8.   These regulations should refer to any general provisions on medical examinations before and during employment and on the prevention of accidents and the protection of health in employment, which may be applicable to the work of seafarers; they should specify measures which will minimize occupational dangers to young seafarers in the course of their duties.

9. (1) Except where a young seafarer is recognized as fully qualified in a pertinent skill by a competent authority, the regulations should specify restrictions on young seafarers undertaking, without appropriate supervision and instruction, certain types of work presenting special risk of accident or of detrimental effect on their health or physical development, or requiring a particular degree of maturity, experience or skill.

(2) In determining the types of work to be restricted by the regulations, the competent authority might consider in particular work involving –

(a) the lifting, moving or carrying of heavy loads or objects;

(b) entry into boilers, tanks and cofferdams;

(c) exposure to harmful noise and vibration levels;

(d) operating hoisting and other power machinery and tools, or acting as signallers to operators of such equipment;

(e) handling mooring or tow lines or ground tackle;

(f) rigging;

(g) work aloft or on deck in heavy weather;

(h) night-watchman duties;

(i) servicing of electrical equipment;

(j) exposure to potentially harmful materials or harmful physical agents such as dangerous or toxic substances, and ionizing radiations;

(k) the cleaning of catering machinery;

(1) the handling or taking charge of ships' boats.

10. Practical measures should be taken by the competent authority or through the appropriate machinery to bring to the attention of young seafarers information concerning the prevention of accidents and the protection of their health in work on board ship, for instance by means of adequate instruction at sea training schools, by official accident-prevention publicity intended for young persons, in the forms indicated in paragraph 8, subparagraph (2), of the Prevention of Accidents (Seafarers) Recommendation, 1970, and by ensuring the professional instruction and supervision of young seafarers in their work in ships.

11. Education and training of young seafarers both ashore and on board ship should include instruction appropriate to their needs in the matters referred to in paragraph 12, clause (f), of the Vocational Training (Seafarers) Recommendation, 1970, and in Regulation 237 of the ILO Model Code of Safety Regulations for Industrial Establishments for the Guidance of Governments and Industry, as amended, as well as guidance on the detrimental effects on their health and well-being of the abuse of drugs and other potentially harmful substances, and of other harmful activities.

VII. OPPORTUNITIES FOR VOCATIONAL GUIDANCE, EDUCATION
AND VOCATIONAL TRAINING

12. The competent authority should, in the light of national conditions, give consideration to the application of the various policies and objectives outlined in paragraphs 13 to 20 below.

13. Young persons should be provided with information concerning training and career opportunities and the conditions of entry into the shipping industry, in accordance with paragraph 7 of the Vocational Training (Seafarers) Recommendation, 1970, as well as regarding shipboard employment and conditions of work, general aspects of collective agreements and seafarers' rights and obligations under maritime labour legislation.

14. Measures should be taken to give young seafarers education, vocational guidance and vocational training in conformity with the objectives specified in paragraph 2 of the Vocational Training (Seafarers) Recommendation, 1970.

15. (1) Initial and further training for occupations in the shipping industry should be broad and comprehensive and should be combined, as appropriate, with further general education.

(2) Such training should combine theoretical instruction with a systematic programme of practical experience designed to prepare for a career within the shipping industry.

(3) Training standards for the seagoing profession should, whenever possible, be coordinated with those applying to occupations ashore so that trainees may acquire nationally recognized qualifications acceptable in both the shipping industry and in other branches of economic activity.

16. Young seafarers should be assisted in receiving education and training for shipboard employment, and subsequently in continuing their general and vocational education, through the various means of financial support specified in paragraph 10, subparagraphs (1) to (5), of the Vocational Training (Seafarers) Recommendation, 1970.

17. The general education and vocational training specified in paragraph 12, clause (g), and paragraph 15 respectively of the Vocational Training (Seafarers) Recommendation, 1970, should be available for all young persons who have no experience of a seagoing ship.

18. Young seafarers should be provided with opportunities for continuing their vocational education and training while on board ship as a means of enabling them to acquire the knowledge and experience essential for the efficient performance of their duties, to qualify for promotion and to pursue their general and technical education. In this regard, ships' masters and officers should encourage and assist young seafarers in applying and fully developing the skills and knowledge gained in induction training, in obtaining appropriate practical experience on board and in pursuing self-study courses at sea.

19.   In addition to the training methods referred to in paragraphs 20 to 25 of the Vocational Training (Seafarers) Recommendation, 1970, young seafarers should have opportunities of –

(a)   continuing their training on board ship by such means as shipboard training, correspondence courses and the provision of programmed instruction and other self-study material in general and nautical subjects designed for the needs of young seafarers in qualifying for promotion;

(b)   pursuing, on board ship, studies to recognized standards in other fields.

20.   Where practicable and possible, training facilities provided for young seafarers on board ship should include accommodation suitable for study purposes, a ship's library, and appropriate training equipment for self-study; young seafarers on board ship should receive special help in their studies, if possible by itinerant instructors embarking periodically.

SAFETY, HEALTH AND WELFARE

Food and Catering (Ships' Crews) Convention, 1946 (No. 68)

Date of entry into force: 24 March 1957

Article 1

1. Every Member of the International Labour Organization for which this Convention is in force is responsible for the promotion of a proper standard of food supply and catering service for the crews of its seagoing vessels, whether publicly or privately owned, which are engaged in the transport of cargo or passengers for the purpose of trade and registered in a territory for which this Convention is in force.

2. National laws or regulations or, in the absence of such laws or regulations, collective agreements between employers and workers, shall determine the vessels or classes of vessels which are to be regarded as seagoing vessels for the purpose of this Convention.

Article 2

The following functions shall be discharged by the competent authority, except in so far as these functions are adequately discharged in virtue of collective agreements –

(a) the framing and enforcement of regulations concerning food and water supplies, catering, and the construction, location, ventilation, heating, lighting, water system and equipment of galleys and other catering department spaces on board ship, including store-rooms and refrigerated chambers;

(b) the inspection of food and water supplies and of the accommodation, arrangements and equipment on board ship for the storage, handling and preparation of food;

(c) the certification of such members of the catering department staff as are required to possess prescribed qualifications;

(d) research into, and educational and propaganda work concerning, methods of ensuring proper food supply and catering service.

Article 3

1.   The competent authority shall work in close cooperation with the organizations of shipowners and seafarers and with national or local authorities concerned with questions of food and health, and may where necessary utilize the services of such authorities.

2.   The activities of the various authorities shall be duly coordinated so as to avoid overlapping or uncertainty of jurisdiction.

Article 4

The competent authority shall have a permanent staff of qualified persons, including inspectors.

Article 5

1.   Each Member shall maintain in force laws or regulations concerning food supply and catering arrangements designed to secure the health and well-being of the crews of the vessels mentioned in Article 1.

2.   These laws or regulations shall require –

(a) the provision of food and water supplies which, having regard to the size of the crew and the duration and nature of the voyage are suitable in respect of quantity, nutritive value, quality and variety;

(b) the arrangement and equipment of the catering department in every vessel in such a manner as to permit of the service of proper meals to the members of the crew.

Article 6

National laws or regulations shall provide for a system of inspection by the competent authority of –

(a) supplies of food and water;

(b) all spaces and equipment used for the storage and handling of food and water;

(c) galley and other equipment for the preparation and service of meals; and

(d) the qualification of such members of the catering department of the crew as are required by such laws or regulations to possess prescribed qualifications.

Article 7

1.   National laws or regulations or, in the absence of such laws or regulations, collective agreements between employers and workers shall provide for inspection at sea at prescribed intervals by the master, or an officer specially deputed for the purpose by him, together with a responsible member of the catering department of:

(a) supplies of food and water;

(b) all spaces and equipment used for the storage and handling of food and water, and galley and other equipment for the preparation and service of meals.

2.   The results of each such inspection shall be recorded.

Article 8

A special inspection shall be made by the representatives of the competent authority of the territory of registration on written complaint made by a number or proportion of the crew prescribed by national laws or regulations or on behalf of a recognized organization of shipowners or seafarers. In order to avoid delay in sailing, such complaints should be submitted as soon as possible and at least twenty-four hours before the scheduled time of departure from port.

Article 9

1.   Inspectors shall have authority to make recommendations to the owner of a ship, or to the master or other person responsible, with a view to the improvement of the standard of catering.

2.   National laws or regulations shall prescribe penalties for –

(a) failure by an owner, master, member of the crew, or other person responsible to comply with the requirements of the national laws or regulations in force; and

(b) any attempt to obstruct an inspector in the discharge of his duties.

3.   Inspectors shall submit regularly to the competent authority reports framed on uniform lines dealing with their work and its results.

Article 10

1.   The competent authority shall prepare an annual report.

2.   The annual report shall be issued as soon as practicable after the end of the year to which it relates and shall be made readily available to all bodies and persons concerned,

3.   Copies of the annual report shall be transmitted to the International Labour Office.

Article 11

1.   Courses of training for employment in the catering department of seagoing ships shall be organized either in approved schools or by means of other arrangements acceptable to both shipowners' and seafarers' organizations.

2.   Facilities shall be provided for refresher courses to enable persons already trained to bring their knowledge and skill up to date.

Article 12

1.   The competent authority shall collect up-to-date information on nutrition and on methods of purchasing, storing, preserving, cooking and serving food, with special reference to the requirements of catering on board ship.

2.   This information shall be made available, free of charge or at reasonable cost, to manufacturers of and traders in ships' food supplies and equipment, ships' masters, stewards and cooks, and shipowners and seafarers and their organizations generally; appropriate forms of publicity, such as manuals, brochures, posters, charts or advertisements in trade journals, shall be used for this purpose.

3.   The competent authority shall issue recommendations to avoid wastage of food, facilitate the maintenance of a proper standard of cleanliness, and ensure the maximum practicable convenience in working.

Article 13

Any of the functions of the competent authority in respect of the certification of catering department staff and the collection and distribution of information may be discharged by delegating the work, or part of it, to a central organization or authority exercising similar functions in respect of seafarers generally.

* * *

Article 15

1.   This Convention shall be binding only upon those Members of the International Labour Organization whose ratifications have been registered with the Director-General.

2.   It shall come into force six months after the date on which there have been registered ratifications by nine of the following countries: United States of America, Argentine Republic, Australia, Belgium, Brazil, Canada, Chile, China, Denmark, Finland, France, United Kingdom of Great Britain and Northern Ireland, Greece, India, Ireland, Italy, Netherlands, Norway, Poland, Portugal, Sweden, Turkey and Yugoslavia, including at least five countries each of which has at least one million gross register tons of shipping. This provision is included for the purpose of facilitating and encouraging early ratification of the Convention by Member States.

3.   Thereafter, this Convention shall come into force for any Member six months after the date on which its ratification has been registered.

Bedding, Mess Utensils and Miscellaneous Provisions (Ships' Crews) Recommendation, 1946 (No. 78)

The Conference recommends that each Member of the International Labour Organization should apply the following principles and should inform the International Labour Office, as requested by the Governing Body, of the measures taken to give effect thereto –

1.   (1)   Clean bedlinen, blankets, bedspreads and mess utensils should be supplied to the members of the crew by the shipowner for use on board during service on the ship, and such members should be responsible for their return at times specified by the master and on completion of service in the ship.

(2)   In the event of any article not being returned in good condition, fair wear and tear excepted, the member of the crew concerned should pay cost price.

2.   Bedlinen, blankets and bedspreads should be of good quality, and plates, cups and other mess utensils should be of approved material which can be easily cleaned.

3.   Towels, soap and toilet paper for the members of the crew should be provided by the shipowner.

Accommodation of Crews Convention (Revised), 1949 (No. 92)

Date of entry into force: 29 January 1953

PART I. GENERAL PROVISIONS

Article 1

1.   This Convention applies to every seagoing mechanically propelled vessel, whether publicly or privately owned, which is engaged in the transport of cargo or passengers for the purpose of trade and is registered in a territory for which this Convention is in force.

2.   National laws or regulations shall determine when vessels are to be regarded as seagoing vessels for the purpose of this Convention.

3.   This Convention does not apply to –

(a) vessels of less than 500 tons;

(b) vessels primarily propelled by sail but having auxiliary engines;

(c) vessels engaged in fishing or in whaling or in similar pursuits;

(d) tugs.

4.   Provided that the Convention shall be applied where reasonable and practicable to –

(a) vessels between 200 and 500 tons; and

(b) the accommodation of persons engaged in usual seagoing routine in vessels engaged in whaling or in similar pursuits.

5.   Provided also that any of the requirements contained in Part III of this Convention may be varied in the case of any ship if the competent authority is satisfied, after consultation with the organizations of shipowners and/or the shipowners and with the bona fide trade unions of seafarers, that the variations to be made provide corresponding advantages as a result of which the overall conditions are not less favourable than those which would result from the full application of the provisions of the Convention; particulars of all such variations shall be communicated by the Member to the Director-General of the International Labour Office, who shall notify the Members of the International Labour Organization,

Article 2

In this Convention –

(a) the term "ship" means a vessel to which the Convention applies;

(b) the term "tons" means gross register tons;

(c) the term "passenger ship" means a ship in respect of which there is in force either (i) a safety certificate issued in accordance with the provisions of the International Convention for the Safety of Life at Sea for the time being in force or (ii) a passenger certificate;

(d) the term "officer" means a person other than a master ranked as an officer by national laws or regulations, or, in the absence of any relevant laws or regulations, by collective agreement or custom;

(e)   the term "rating" means a member of the crew other than an officer;

(f)   the term "petty officer" means a rating serving in a supervisory position or position of special responsibility who is classed as petty officer by national laws or regulations, or, in the absence of any relevant laws or regulations, by collective agreement or custom;

(g)   the term "crew accommodation" includes such sleeping rooms, mess rooms, sanitary accommodation, hospital accommodation and recreation accommodation as are provided for the use of the crew;

(h)   the term "prescribed" means prescribed by national laws or regulations or by the competent authority;

(i)   the term "approved" means approved by the competent authority;

(j)   the term "re-registered" means re-registered on the occasion of a simultaneous change in the territory of registration and ownership of the vessel.

Article 3

1.   Each Member for which this Convention is in force undertakes to maintain in force laws or regulations which ensure the application of the provisions of Parts II, III and IV of this Convention.

2.   The laws or regulations shall –

(a)   require the competent authority to bring them to the notice of all persons concerned;

(b)   define the persons responsible for compliance therewith;

(c)   prescribe adequate penalties for any violation thereof;

(d)   provide for the maintenance of a system of inspection adequate to ensure effective enforcement;

(e)   require the competent authority to consult the organizations of shipowners and/or the shipowners and the recognized bona fide trade unions of seafarers in regard to the framing of regulations, and to collaborate so far as practicable with such parties in the administration thereof.

PART II. PLANNING AND CONTROL OF CREW ACCOMMODATION

Article 4

1.   Before the construction of a ship is begun a plan of the ship, showing on a prescribed scale the location and general arrangement of the crew accommodation, shall be submitted for approval to the competent authority.

2.   Before the construction of the crew accommodation is begun and before the crew accommodation in an existing ship is altered or reconstructed, detailed plans of, and information concerning, the accommodation, showing on a prescribed scale and in prescribed detail the allocation of each space, the disposition of furniture and fittings, the means and arrangement of ventilation, lighting and heating, and the sanitary arrangements, shall be submitted for approval to the competent authority: Provided that in the case of emergency or temporary altera-

tions or reconstruction effected outside the territory of registration it shall be sufficient compliance with this provision if the plans are subsequently submitted for approval to the competent authority.

Article 5

On every occasion when –

(a) a ship is registered or re-registered,

(b) the crew accommodation of a ship has been substantially altered or reconstructed, or

(c) complaint has been made to the competent authority in the prescribed manner and in time to prevent any delay to the vessel by a recognized bona fide trade union of seafarers representing all or part of the crew or by a prescribed number or proportion of the members of the crew of the ship that the crew accommodation is not in compliance with the terms of this Convention,

the competent authority shall inspect the ship and satisfy itself that the crew accommodation complies with the requirements of the laws and regulations.

PART III. CREW ACCOMMODATION REQUIREMENTS

Article 6

1.   The location, means of access, structure and arrangement in relation to other spaces of crew accommodation shall be such as to ensure adequate security, protection against weather and sea, and insulation from heat or cold, undue noise or effluvia from other spaces.

2.   There shall be no direct openings into sleeping rooms from spaces for cargo and machinery or from galleys, lamp and paint rooms or from engine, deck and other bulk storerooms, drying rooms, communal wash places or water closets. That part of the bulkhead separating such places from sleeping rooms and external bulkheads shall be efficiently constructed of steel or other approved substance and shall be watertight and gastight.

3.   External bulkheads of sleeping rooms and mess rooms shall be adequately insulated. All machinery casings and all boundary bulkheads of galleys and other spaces in which heat is produced shall be adequately insulated where there is a possibility of resulting heat effects in adjoining accommodation or passageways, Care shall also be taken to provide protection from heat effects of steam and/or hot-water service pipes,

4.   Internal bulkheads shall be of approved material which is not likely to harbour vermin.

5.   Sleeping rooms, mess rooms, recreation rooms and alleyways in the crew accommodation space shall be adequately insulated to prevent condensation or overheating.

6.   Main steam and exhaust pipes for winches and similar gear shall not pass through crew accommodation nor, whenever technically possible, through

alley-ways leading to crew accommodation; where they do pass through such alley-ways they shall be adequately insulated and encased.

7.   Inside panelling or sheeting shall be of material with a surface easily kept clean. Tongued and grooved boarding or any other form of construction likely to harbour vermin shall not be used.

8.   The competent authority shall decide to what extent fire-prevention or fire-retarding measures shall be required to be taken in the construction of the accommodation.

9.   The wall surface and deckheads in sleeping rooms and mess rooms shall be capable of being easily kept clean and, if painted, shall be light in colour; lime wash must not be used.

10.   The wall surfaces shall be renewed or restored as necessary.

11.   The decks in all crew accommodation shall be of approved material and construction and shall provide a surface impervious to damp and easily kept clean.

12.   Where the floorings are of composition the joinings with sides shall be rounded to avoid crevices.

13.   Sufficient drainage shall be provided.

Article 7

1.   Sleeping rooms and mess rooms shall be adequately ventilated.

2.   The system of ventilation shall be controlled so as to maintain the air in a satisfactory condition and to ensure a sufficiency of air movement in all conditions of weather and climate.

3.   Ships regularly engaged on voyages in the tropics and the Persian Gulf shall be equipped with both mechanical means of ventilation and electric fans: Provided that one only of these means need be adopted in spaces where this ensures satisfactory ventilation.

4.   Ships engaged outside the tropics shall be equipped with either mechanical means of ventilation or electric fans. The competent authority may exempt ships normally employed in the cold waters of the northern or southern hemispheres from this requirement.

5.   Power for the operation of the aids to ventilation required by paragraphs 3 and 4 shall, when practicable, be available at all times when the crew is living or working on board and conditions so require.

Article 8

1.   An adequate system of heating the crew accommodation shall be provided except in ships engaged exclusively in voyages in the tropics and the Persian Gulf.

2.   The heating system shall, when practicable, be in operation at all times when the crew is living or working on board and conditions require its use.

3.   In all ships in which a heating system is required, the heating shall be by means of steam, hot water, warm air or electricity.

4. In any ships in which heating is provided by a stove, measures shall be taken to ensure that the stove is of sufficient size and is properly installed and guarded and that the air is not fouled.

5. The heating system shall be capable of maintaining the temperature in crew accommodation at a satisfactory level under normal conditions of weather and climate likely to be met with on service; the competent authority shall prescribe the standard to be provided.

6. Radiators and other heating apparatus shall be so placed and, where necessary, shielded as to avoid risk of fire or danger or discomfort to the occupants.

Article 9

1. Subject to such special arrangements as may be permitted in passenger ships, sleeping rooms and mess rooms shall be properly lighted by natural light and shall be provided with adequate artificial light.

2. All crew spaces shall be adequately lighted. The minimum standard for natural lighting in living rooms shall be such as to permit a person with a normal vision to read on a clear day an ordinary newspaper in any part of the space available for free movement. When it is not possible to provide adequate natural lighting, artificial lighting of the above minimum standard shall be provided.

3. In all ships electric lights shall be provided in the crew accommodation, If there are not two independent sources of electricity for lighting, additional lighting shall be provided by properly constructed lamps or lighting apparatus for emergency use.

4. Artificial lighting shall be so disposed as to give the maximum benefit to the occupants of the room.

5. In sleeping rooms an electric reading lamp shall be installed at the head of each berth.

Article 10

1. Sleeping rooms shall be situated above the load line amidships or aft.

2. In exceptional cases the competent authority may, if the size, type or intended service of the ship render any other location unreasonable or impracticable, permit the location of sleeping rooms in the fore part of the ship, but in no case forward of the collision bulkhead.

3. In passenger ships the competent authority may, on condition that satisfactory arrangements are made for lighting and ventilation, permit the location of sleeping rooms below the load line, but in no case immediately beneath working alley-ways.

4. The floor area per person of sleeping rooms intended for ratings shall be not less than –

(a) 20 sq. ft. or 1.85 sq. m. in vessels under 800 tons;

(b) 25 sq. ft. or 2.35 sq. m. in vessels of 800 tons or over, but under 3,000 tons;

(c) 30 sq. ft. or 2.78 sq. m. in vessels of 3,000 tons or over:

Provided that, in the case of passenger ships in which more than four ratings are berthed in one room, the minimum per person may be 24 sq. ft. (2.22 sq. m.).

5. In the case of ships in which are employed such groups of ratings as necessitate the employment of a substantially larger number of ratings than would otherwise be employed, the competent authority may, in respect of such groups, reduce the minimum floor area of sleeping rooms per person, subject to the conditions that –

(a) the total sleeping space allotted to the group or groups is not less than would have been allotted had the numbers not been so increased, and

(b) the minimum floor area of sleeping rooms is not less than –

   (i) 18 sq. ft. (1.67 sq. m.) per person in ships under 3,000 tons;

   (ii) 20 sq. ft. (1.85 sq. m.) per person in ships of 3,000 tons or over.

6. Space occupied by berths and lockers, chests of drawers and seats shall be included in the measurement of the floor area. Small or irregularly shaped spaces which do not add effectively to the space available for free movement and cannot be used for installing furniture shall be excluded.

7. The clear head room in crew sleeping rooms shall not be less than 6 ft. 3 ins (190 cm.).

8. There shall be a sufficient number of sleeping rooms to provide a separate room or rooms for each department: Provided that the competent authority may relax this requirement in the case of small ships.

9. The number of persons allowed to occupy sleeping rooms shall not exceed the following maxima:

(a) officers in charge of a department, navigating and engineer officers in charge of a watch and senior radio officers or operators: one person per room;

(b) other officers: one person per room wherever possible, and in no case more than two;

(c) petty officers: one or two persons per room, and in no case more than two;

(d) other ratings: two or three persons per room wherever possible, and in no case more than four.

10. With a view to ensuring adequate and more comfortable accommodation the competent authority may, after consultation with the organizations of shipowners and/or the shipowners and the bona fide trade unions of seafarers, grant permission to accommodate up to ten ratings per sleeping room in the case of certain passenger ships.

11. The maximum number of persons to be accommodated in any sleeping room shall be indelibly and legibly marked in some place in the room where it can conveniently be seen.

12. Members of the crew shall be provided with individual berths.

13. Berths shall not be placed side by side in such a way that access to one berth can be obtained only over another.

14.   Berths shall not be arranged in tiers of more than two; in the case of berths placed along the ship's side, there shall be only a single tier where a side-light is situated above a berth.

15.   The lower berth in a double tier shall be not less than 12 ins. (30 cm.) above the floor; the upper berth shall be placed approximately midway between the bottom of the lower berth and the lower side of the deckhead beams.

16.   The minimum inside dimensions of a berth shall be 6 ft. 3 ins. by 2 ft. 3 ins. (190 cm. by 68 cm.).

17.   The framework and the lee-board, if any, of a berth shall be of approved material, hard, smooth, and not likely to corrode or to harbour vermin.

18.   If tubular frames are used for the construction of berths, they shall be completely sealed and without perforations which would give access to vermin.

19.   Each berth shall be fitted with a spring bottom or a spring mattress and with a mattress of approved material. Stuffing of straw or other material likely to harbour vermin shall not be used.

20.   When one berth is placed over another a dust-proof bottom of wood, canvas or other suitable material shall be fitted beneath the spring bottom of the upper berth.

21.   Sleeping rooms shall be so planned and equipped as to ensure reasonable comfort for the occupants and to facilitate tidiness.

22.   The furniture shall include a clothes locker for each occupant. The clothes lockers shall be not less than 5 ft. (152 cm.) in height and of a cross-section area of 300 sq. ins. (19.30 sq. decimeters) and shall be fitted with a shelf and a hasp for a padlock. The padlock shall be provided by the occupant.

23.   Each sleeping room shall be provided with a table or desk, which may be of the fixed, drop-leaf or slide-out type, and with comfortable seating accommodation as necessary.

24.   The furniture shall be of smooth, hard material not liable to warp or corrode.

25.   The drawer or equivalent space for each occupant shall be not less than 2 cu. ft. (.056 cu. m.).

26.   Sleeping rooms shall be fitted with curtains for the side-lights.

27.   Sleeping rooms shall be fitted with a mirror, small cabinets for toilet requisites, a book rack and a sufficient number of coat hooks.

28.   As far as practicable, berthing of crew members shall be so arranged that watches are separated and that no daymen share a room with watch-keepers.

Article 11

1.   Sufficient mess room accommodation shall be provided in all ships.

2.   In ships of less than 1,000 tons separate mess room accommodation shall be provided for –

(a)   master and officers;

(b) petty officers and other ratings.

3.   In ships of 1,000 tons and over, separate mess room accommodation shall be provided for –

(a) master and officers;

(b) deck department petty officers and other ratings;

(c) engine department petty officers and other ratings;

Provided that

(i)   one of the two mess rooms for the petty officers and other ratings may be allotted to the petty officers and the other to the other ratings;

(ii) a single mess room may be provided for deck and engine department petty officers and other ratings in cases in which the organizations of shipowners and/or shipowners and the recognized bona fide trade unions of seafarers concerned have expressed a preference for such an arrangement.

4.   Adequate mess room accommodation shall be provided for the catering department, either by the provision of a separate mess room or by giving them the right to the use of the mess rooms assigned to other groups; in the case of ships of 5,000 tons or over with more than five persons in the catering department, consideration shall be given to the provision of a separate mess room,

5.   The dimensions and equipment of each mess room shall be sufficient for the number of persons likely to use it at any one time.

6.   Mess rooms shall be equipped with tables and approved seats sufficient for the number of persons likely to use them at any one time.

7.   The competent authority may permit such exceptions to the foregoing rules concerning mess room accommodation as may be necessary to meet the special conditions in passenger ships.

8.   Mess rooms shall be located apart from the sleeping rooms and as close as practicable to the galley.

9.   Where available pantries are not accessible to mess rooms, adequate lockers for mess utensils and proper facilities for washing utensils shall be provided.

10.   The tops of tables and seats shall be of damp-resisting material, without cracks and capable of being easily cleaned.

Article 12

1.   In all ships a space or spaces to which the crew can have access when off duty shall be provided on an open deck; the space or spaces shall be of adequate area, having regard to the size of the ship and the crew.

2.   Recreation accommodation, conveniently situated and appropriately furnished, shall be provided for officers and for ratings. Where this is not provided separately from the mess rooms the latter shall be planned, furnished, and equipped to give recreational facilities.

Article 13

1. Sufficient sanitary accommodation, including wash basins and tub and/or shower baths, shall be provided in all ships.

2. The following minimum number of separate water closets shall be provided –

(a) in ships of under 800 tons: three;

(b) in ships of 800 tons or over, but under 3,000 tons: four;

(c) in ships of 3,000 tons or over: six;

(d) in ships where the radio officers or operators are accommodated in an isolated position, sanitary facilities near or adjacent thereto shall be provided.

3. National laws or regulations shall prescribe the allocation of water closets to various groups, subject to the provisions of paragraph 4 of this Article.

4. Sanitary facilities for all members of the crew who do not occupy rooms to which private facilities are attached shall be provided for each group of the crew on the following scale –

(a) one tub and/or shower bath for every eight persons or less;

(b) one water closet for every eight persons or less;

(c) one wash basin for every six persons or less;

Provided that when the number of persons in a group exceeds an even multiple of the specified number by less than one-half of the specified number this surplus may be ignored for the purpose of this paragraph.

5. When the total number of the crew exceeds 100 and in passenger vessels normally engaged on voyages of not more than four hours' duration, consideration may be given by the competent authority to special arrangements or a reduction in the number of facilities required.

6. Cold fresh water and hot fresh water or means of heating water shall be available in all communal wash places. The competent authority, in consultation with the organizations of shipowners and/or the shipowners and with the recognized bona fide trade unions of seafarers, may fix the maximum amount of fresh water which the shipowner may be required to supply per man per day.

7. Wash basins and tub baths shall be of adequate size and constructed of approved material with a smooth surface not liable to crack, flake or corrode.

8. All water closets shall have ventilation to the open air, independently of any other part of the accommodation.

9. All water closets shall be of an approved pattern and provided with an ample flush of water, available at all times and independently controllable.

10. Soil pipes and waste pipes shall be of adequate dimensions and shall be so constructed as to minimize the risk of obstruction and to facilitate cleaning.

11. Sanitary accommodation intended for the use of more than one person shall comply with the following requirements:

(a) floors shall be of approved durable material, easily cleaned and impervious to damp, and shall be properly drained;

(b) bulkheads shall be of steel or other approved material and shall be watertight up to at least 9 ins. (23 cm.) above the level of the deck;

(c) the accommodation shall be sufficiently lighted, heated and ventilated;

(d) water closets shall be situated convenient to, but separate from, sleeping rooms and wash rooms, without direct access from the sleeping rooms or from a passage between sleeping rooms and water closets to which there is no other access: Provided that this requirement shall not apply where a water closet is located in a compartment between two sleeping rooms having a total of not more than four persons;

(e) where there is more than one water closet in a compartment, they shall be sufficiently screened to ensure privacy.

12. In all ships facilities for washing and drying clothes shall be provided on a scale appropriate to the size of the crew and the normal duration of the voyage.

13. The facilities for washing clothes shall include suitable sinks, which may be installed in wash rooms, if separate laundry accommodation is not reasonably practicable, with an adequate supply of cold fresh water and hot fresh water or means of heating water.

14. The facilities for drying clothes shall be provided in a compartment separate from sleeping rooms and mess rooms, adequately ventilated and heated and equipped with lines or other fittings for hanging clothes.

Article 14

1. In any ship carrying a crew of fifteen or more and engaged in a voyage of more than three days' duration, separate hospital accommodation shall be provided. The competent authority may relax this requirement in respect of vessels engaged in coastal trade.

2. The hospital accommodation shall be suitably situated, so that it is easy of access and so that the occupants may be comfortably housed and may receive proper attention in all weathers.

3. The arrangement of the entrance, berths, lighting, ventilation, heating and water supply shall be designed to ensure the comfort and facilitate the treatment of the occupants.

4. The number of hospital berths required shall be prescribed by the competent authority.

5. Water closet accommodation shall be provided for the exclusive use of the occupants of the hospital accommodation, either as part of the accommodation or in close proximity thereto.

6. Hospital accommodation shall not be used for other than medical purposes.

7. An approved medicine chest with readily understandable instructions shall be carried in every ship which does not carry a doctor.

Article 15

1.   Sufficiently and adequately ventilated accommodation for the hanging of oilskins shall be provided outside but convenient to the sleeping rooms.

2.   In ships of over 3,000 tons one room for the deck department and one room for the engine department shall be provided and equipped for use as an office.

3.   In ships regularly trading to mosquito-infested ports provision shall be made to protect the crews' quarters against the admission of mosquitoes by the fitting of suitable screens to side scuttles, ventilators and doors to the open deck.

4.   All ships trading regularly to or in the tropics and the Persian Gulf shall be equipped with awnings for use over exposed decks above crew accommodation and over recreation deck space or spaces.

Article 16

1.   In the case of the ships mentioned in paragraph 5 of Article 10 the competent authority may, in respect of the members of the crew there referred to, modify the requirements laid down in the foregoing articles as far as may be necessary to take account of their distinctive national habits and customs and in particular may make special arrangements concerning the number of persons occupying sleeping rooms and concerning mess room and sanitary facilities.

2.   In modifying the said requirements the competent authority shall be bound by the specifications set forth in paragraphs 1 and 2 of Article 10 and by the minimum sleeping space requirements prescribed for such groups of ratings in paragraph 5 of Article 10.

3.   In ships in which the crew in any department are persons of widely different national habits and customs, separate and appropriate sleeping and living accommodation shall be provided as may be necessary to meet the requirements of the different groups.

4.   In the case of the ships mentioned in paragraph 5 of Article 10 the hospital, dining, bathing and sanitary facilities shall be provided and maintained on a standard, in regard to their quantity and practical usefulness, equal or comparable to that which obtains aboard all other ships of similar type and belonging to the same registry.

5.   The competent authority shall, when framing special regulations under this Article, consult the recognized bona fide trade unions of seafarers concerned and the organizations of shipowners and/or the shipowners employing them.

Article 17

1.   Crew accommodation shall be maintained in a clean and decently habitable condition and shall be kept free of goods and stores not the personal property of the occupants.

2.   The master, or an officer specially deputed for the purpose by him, accompanied by one or more members of the crew, shall inspect all crew accommodation at intervals of not more than one week. The results of each such inspection shall be recorded.

PART IV. APPLICATION OF CONVENTION TO EXISTING SHIPS

Article 18

1.   Subject to the provisions of paragraphs 2, 3 and 4 of this Article, this Convention applies to ships the keels of which are laid down subsequent to the coming into force of the Convention for the territory of registration.

2.   In the case of a ship which is fully complete on the date of the coming into force of this Convention for the territory of registration and which is below the standard set by Part III of this Convention, the competent authority may, after consultation with the organizations of shipowners and/or the shipowners and with the bona fide trade unions of seafarers, require such alterations for the purpose of bringing the ship into conformity with the requirements of the Convention as it deems possible, having regard to the practical problems involved, to be made when –

(a)   the ship is re-registered;

(b)   substantial structural alterations or major repairs are made to the vessel as a result of long-range plans and not as a result of an accident or emergency.

3.   In the case of a ship in the process of building and/or reconversion on the date of the coming into force of this Convention for the territory of registration, the competent authority may, after consultation with the organizations of shipowners and/or the shipowners and with the bona fide trade unions of seafarers, require such alterations for the purpose of bringing the ship into conformity with the requirements of the Convention as it deems possible having regard to the practical problems involved; such alterations shall constitute final compliance with the terms of this Convention, unless and until the ship be re-registered.

4.   In the case of a ship, other than such a ship as is referred to in paragraphs 2 and 3 of this Article or a ship to which the provisions of this Convention were applicable while she was under construction, being re-registered in a territory after the date of the coming into force of this Convention for that territory, the competent authority may, after consultation with the organizations of shipowners and/or the shipowners and with the bona fide trade unions of seafarers, require such alterations for the purpose of bringing the ship into conformity with the requirements of the Convention as it deems possible having regard to the practical problems involved; such alterations shall constitute final compliance with the terms of this Convention, unless and until the ship is again re-registered.

Article 19

Nothing in this Convention shall affect any law, award, custom or agreement between shipowners and seafarers which ensures more favourable conditions than those provided for by this Convention.

* * *

Article 21

1.   This Convention shall be binding only upon those Members of the International Labour Organization whose ratifications have been registered with the Director-General.

2.   It shall come into force six months after the date on which there have been registered ratifications by seven of the following countries: United States of America, Argentine Republic, Australia, Belgium, Brazil, Canada, Chile, China, Denmark, Finland, France, United Kingdom of Great Britain and Northern Ireland, Greece, India, Ireland, Italy, Netherlands, Norway, Poland, Portugal, Sweden, Turkey and Yugoslavia, including at least four countries each of which has at least one million gross register tons of shipping. This provision is included for the purpose of facilitating and encouraging early ratification of the Convention by member States.

3.   Thereafter, this Convention shall come into force for any Member six months after the date on which its ratification has been registered.

Accommodation of Crews (Supplementary Provisions) Convention, 1970 (No. 133)

Date of entry into force: 27 August 1991

PART I. GENERAL PROVISIONS

Article 1

1.   This Convention applies to every seagoing ship, whether publicly or privately owned, which is engaged in the transport of cargo or passengers for the purpose of trade or is employed for any other commercial purpose, which is registered in a territory for which this Convention is in force, and of which the keel is laid, or which is at a similar stage of construction, on or after the date of coming into force of the Convention for that territory.

2.   National laws or regulations shall determine when ships are to be regarded as seagoing ships for the purpose of this Convention.

3.   This Convention applies to tugs where reasonable and practicable.

4.   This Convention does not apply to –

(a) ships of less than 1,000 tons;

(b) ships primarily propelled by sail, whether or not they are fitted with auxiliary engines;

(c) ships engaged in fishing or in whaling or in similar pursuits;

(d) hydrofoils and air-cushion craft.

5.   Provided that the Convention shall be applied where reasonable and practicable to –

(a) ships between 200 and 1,000 tons; and

(b) the accommodation of persons engaged in usual seagoing routine in ships engaged in whaling or in similar pursuits.

6.   Provided also that any of the requirements applicable by virtue of Article 3 of this Convention may be varied in the case of any ship if the competent authority is satisfied, after consultation with the organizations of shipowners and/or the shipowners and with the bona fide trade unions of seafarers, that the variations

to be made provide corresponding advantages as a result of which the overall conditions are not less favourable than those which would result from the full application of the provisions of the Convention; particulars of all such variations shall be communicated by the Member concerned to the Director-General of the International Labour Office.

7.　Provided further that the competent authority shall, after consultation with the organizations of shipowners and/or the shipowners and with the bona fide trade unions of seafarers, determine the extent to which it is appropriate, taking into consideration the need for off-duty accommodation, to make exceptions or to diverge from the provisions of this Convention in the case of –

(a) seagoing ferries, feeder ships and similar ships which are not continuously manned with one permanent crew;

(b) seagoing ships when repair personnel are carried temporarily in addition to the ship's crew;

(c) seagoing ships engaged on short voyages which allow members of the crew to go home or to make use of comparable facilities for part of each day.

Article 2

In this Convention –

(a) the term "ship" means a vessel to which the Convention applies;

(b) the term "tons" means gross register tons;

(c) the term "passenger ship" means a ship in respect of which there is in force either (i) a passenger ship safety certificate issued in accordance with the provisions of the International Convention for the Safety of Life at Sea for the time being in force, or (ii) a passenger certificate;

(d) the term "officer" means a person other than a master ranked as an officer by national laws or regulations, or, in the absence of any relevant laws or regulations, by collective agreement or custom;

(e) the term "rating" means a member of the crew other than an officer;

(f) the term "petty officer" means a rating serving in a supervisory position or position of special responsibility who is classed as petty officer by national laws or regulations, or, in the absence of any relevant laws or regulations, by collective agreement or custom;

(g) the term "adult" means a person who is at least 18 years of age;

(h) the term "crew accommodation" includes such sleeping rooms, mess rooms, sanitary accommodation, hospital accommodation and recreation accommodation as are provided for the use of the crew;

(i) the term "prescribed" means prescribed by national laws or regulations or by the competent authority;

(j) the term "approved" means approved by the competent authority;

(k) the term "re-registered" means re-registered on the occasion of a simultaneous change in the territory of registration and ownership of the ship.

Article 3

Each Member for which this Convention is in force undertakes to comply, in respect of ships to which this Convention applies, with –

(a) the provisions of Parts II and III of the Accommodation of Crews Convention (Revised), 1949; and

(b) the provisions of Part II of this Convention.

Article 4

1. Each Member for which this Convention is in force undertakes to maintain in force laws or regulations which ensure its application.

2. The laws or regulations shall –

(a) require the competent authority to bring them to the notice of all persons concerned;

(b) define the persons responsible for compliance therewith;

(c) prescribe adequate penalties for any violation thereof;

(d) provide for the maintenance of a system of inspection adequate to ensure effective enforcement;

(e) require the competent authority to consult the organizations of shipowners and/or the shipowners and the bona fide trade unions of seafarers in regard to the framing of regulations, and to collaborate so far as practicable with such parties in the administration thereof.

PART II. CREW ACCOMMODATION REQUIREMENTS

Article 5

1. The floor area per person of sleeping rooms intended for ratings shall be not less than –

(a) 3.75 square metres (40.36 square feet) in ships of 1,000 tons or over but less than 3,000 tons;

(b) 4.25 square metres (45.75 square feet) in ships of 3,000 tons or over but less than 10,000 tons;

(c) 4.75 square metres (51.13 square feet) in ships of 10,000 tons or over.

2. Provided that the floor area per person of sleeping rooms intended for two ratings shall be not less than –

(a) 2.75 square metres (29.60 square feet) in ships of 1,000 tons or over but less than 3,000 tons;

(b) 3.25 square metres (34.98 square feet) in ships of 3,000 tons or over but less than 10,000 tons;

(c) 3.75 square metres (40.36 square feet) in ships of 10,000 tons or over.

3. Provided also that the floor area of sleeping rooms intended for ratings in passenger ships shall be not less than –

(a) 2.35 square metres (25.30 square feet) per person in ships of 1,000 tons or over but less than 3,000 tons;

(b) in ships of 3,000 tons or over –

   (i) 3.75 square metres (40.36 square feet) in rooms accommodating one person;

   (ii) 6.00 square metres (64.58 square feet) in rooms accommodating two persons;

   (iii) 9.00 square metres (96.88 square feet) in rooms accommodating three persons;

   (iv) 12.00 square metres (129.17 square feet) in rooms accommodating four persons.

4. The number of ratings occupying sleeping rooms shall not exceed two persons per room, except in passenger ships where the maximum number permissible shall be four.

5. The number of petty officers occupying sleeping rooms shall not exceed one or two persons per room.

6. In sleeping rooms for officers, where no private sitting room or day room is provided, the floor area per person shall be not less than 6.50 square metres (69.96 square feet) in ships of less than 3,000 tons, and not less than 7.50 square metres (80.73 square feet) in ships of 3,000 tons or over.

7. In ships other than passenger ships an individual sleeping room shall be provided for each adult member of the crew, where the size of the ship, the activity in which it is to be engaged, and its layout make this reasonable and practicable.

8. Where practicable in ships of 3,000 tons or over, the chief engineer officer and the chief navigating officer shall have, in addition to their sleeping room, an adjoining sitting room or day room.

9. Space occupied by berths and lockers, chests of drawers and seats shall be included in the measurement of the floor area. Small or irregularly shaped spaces which do not add effectively to the space available for free movement and cannot be used for installing furniture shall be excluded.

10. The minimum inside dimensions of a berth shall be 198 centimetres by 80 centimetres (6 feet 6 inches by 2 feet 7.50 inches).

Article 6

1. The floor area of mess rooms for officers and for ratings shall be not less than 1 square metre (10.76 square feet) per person of the planned seating capacity.

2. Mess rooms shall be equipped with tables and approved seats, fixed or movable, sufficient to accommodate the greatest number of members of the crew likely to use them at any one time.

3. There shall be available at all times when members of the crew are on board –

(a) a refrigerator, which shall be conveniently situated, of sufficient capacity for the number of persons using the mess room or mess rooms;

(b) facilities for hot beverages; and

(c) cool water facilities.

4.   The competent authority may permit such exceptions to the provisions of paragraphs 1 and 2 of this Article concerning mess room accommodation as may be necessary to meet the special conditions in passenger ships.

Article 7

1.   Recreation accommodation, conveniently situated and appropriately furnished, shall be provided for officers and for ratings. Where this is not provided separately from the mess rooms the latter shall be planned, furnished and equipped to give recreational facilities.

2.   Furnishings for recreation accommodation shall as a minimum include a bookcase and facilities for reading, writing and, where practicable, for games.

3.   In respect of ships of 8,000 tons or over, a smoking room or library room in which films or television may be shown and a hobby and games room shall be provided; consideration shall be given to the provision of a swimming pool.

4.   In connection with the planning of recreation accommodation, the competent authority shall give consideration to the provision of a canteen.

Article 8

1.   In all ships a minimum of one water closet and one tub and/or shower bath for every six persons or less who do not have facilities in pursuance of paragraphs 2 to 4 of this Article shall be provided at a convenient location for officers and for ratings. When women are employed in a ship, separate sanitary facilities shall be provided for them.

2.   In ships of 5,000 tons or over but less than 15,000 tons, individual sleeping rooms for at least five officers shall have attached to them a separate private bathroom fitted with a water closet as well as a tub and/or shower bath and a wash basin having hot and cold running fresh water; the wash basin may be situated in the sleeping room. In addition, in ships of 10,000 tons or over but less than 15,000 tons, the sleeping rooms of all other officers shall have private or intercommunicating bathrooms similarly fitted.

3.   In ships of 15,000 tons or over, individual sleeping rooms for officers shall have attached to them a separate private bathroom fitted with a water closet as well as a tub and/or shower bath and a wash basin having hot and cold running fresh water; the wash basin may be situated in the sleeping room.

4.   In ships of 25,000 tons or over, other than passenger ships, a bathroom for every two ratings shall be provided, either in an intercommunicating compartment between adjoining sleeping rooms or opposite the entrance of such rooms, which shall be fitted with a water closet as well as a tub and/or shower bath and a wash basin having hot and cold running fresh water.

5.   In ships of 5,000 tons or over, other than passenger ships, each sleeping room, whether for officers or ratings, shall be provided with a wash basin having hot and cold running fresh water, except where such wash basin is situated in a bathroom provided in conformity with paragraphs 2, 3 or 4 of this Article.

6.   In all ships, facilities for washing, drying and ironing clothes shall be provided for officers and ratings on a scale appropriate to the size of the crew and the normal duration of the voyage. These facilities shall, whenever possible, be located within easy access of their accommodation.

7.   The facilities to be provided shall be –

(a) washing machines;

(b) drying machines or adequately heated and ventilated drying rooms; and

(c) irons and ironing boards or their equivalent.

Article 9

1.   In ships of 1,600 tons or over there shall be provided –

(a) a separate compartment containing a water closet and a wash basin having hot and cold running fresh water, within easy access of the navigating bridge deck primarily for those on duty in the area; and

(b) a water closet and a wash basin having hot and cold running fresh water, within easy access of the machinery space if not fitted near the engine room control centre.

2.   In ships of 1,600 tons or over, other than ships in which private sleeping rooms and private or semi-private bathrooms are provided for all engine department personnel, facilities for changing clothes shall be provided which shall be –

(a) located outside the machinery space but with easy access to it; and

(b) fitted with individual clothes lockers as well as with tubs and/or shower baths and wash basins having hot and cold running fresh water.

Article 10

The minimum headroom in all crew accommodation where full and free movement is necessary shall be not less than 198 centimetres (6 feet 6 inches): Provided that the competent authority may permit some limited reduction in headroom in any space, or part of any space, in such accommodation where it is satisfied that it is reasonable to do so and also that such reduction will not result in discomfort to the crew.

Article 11

1.   Crew accommodation shall be properly lighted.

2.   Subject to such special arrangements as may be permitted in passenger ships, sleeping rooms and mess rooms shall be lighted by natural light and shall be provided with adequate artificial light.

3.   In all ships electric light shall be provided in the crew accommodation. If there are not two independent sources of electricity for lighting, additional light-

ing shall be provided by properly constructed lamps or lighting apparatus for emergency use.

4.   In sleeping rooms an electric reading lamp shall be installed at the head of each berth.

5.   Suitable standards of natural and artificial lighting shall be fixed by the competent authority.

Article 12

In the case of ships the manning of which has to take account, without discrimination, of the interests of crews having differing and distinctive religious and social practices, the competent authority may, after consultation with the organizations of shipowners and/or the shipowners and with the bona fide trade unions of the seafarers concerned, and provided that these two sides are in agreement, permit variations in respect of the provisions of paragraphs 1 to 4 and paragraph 7 of Article 5 and paragraphs 1 and 4 of Article 8 of this Convention on condition that such variations do not result in over-all facilities less favourable than those which would result from the application of the provisions of the Convention. Particulars of all such variations shall be communicated by the Member concerned to the Director-General of the International Labour Office who shall notify the Members of the International Labour Organization.

PART III.   APPLICATION OF THE CONVENTION TO EXISTING SHIPS

Article 13

1.   In the case of a ship which is fully complete on the date of the coming into force of this Convention for the territory of registration and which is below the standard set by this Convention, the competent authority may, after consultation with the organizations of shipowners and/or the shipowners and with the bona fide trade unions of seafarers, require such alterations for the purpose of bringing the ship into conformity with the requirements of the Convention as it deems reasonable and practicable, having regard in particular to technical, economic and other problems involved in the application of Articles 5, 8 and 10, to be made when –

(a)   the ship is re-registered;

(b)   substantial structural alterations or major repairs are made to the ship as a result of long-range plans and not as a consequence of an accident or emergency.

2.   In the case of a ship in the process of building and/or conversion on the date of the coming into force of this Convention for the territory of registration, the competent authority may, after consultation with the organizations of shipowners and/or the shipowners and with the bona fide trade unions of seafarers, require such alterations for the purpose of bringing the ship into conformity with the requirements of the Convention as it deems reasonable and practicable, having regard in particular to technical, economic and other problems involved in the

application of Articles 5, 8 and 10; such alterations shall constitute final compliance with the terms of this Convention.

3.   In the case of a ship, other than such a ship as is referred to in paragraphs 1 and 2 of this Article or a ship to which the provisions of this Convention were applicable while she was under construction, being re-registered in a territory after the date of the coming into force of this Convention for that territory, the competent authority may, after consultation with the organizations of shipowners and/or the shipowners and with the bona fide trade unions of seafarers, require such alterations for the purpose of bringing the ship into conformity with the requirements of the Convention as it deems reasonable and practicable, having regard in particular to technical, economic and other problems involved in the application of Articles 5, 8 and 10; such alterations shall constitute final compliance with the terms of this Convention.

* * *

Article 15

1.   This Convention shall be binding only upon those Members of the International Labour Organization whose ratifications have been registered with the Director-General.

2.   It shall come into force twelve months after the date on which there have been registered ratifications by twelve Members each of which has more than one million tons of shipping, including at least four Members each of which has at least two million tons of shipping.

3.   Thereafter, this Convention shall come into force for any Member six months after the date on which its ratification has been registered.

Crew Accommodation (Air Conditioning) Recommendation, 1970 (No. 140)

1.   (1)   All ships of 1,000 gross register tons or over constructed after the adoption of this Recommendation, except those regularly engaged in trades where temperate climatic conditions do not require this, should be equipped with air conditioning of crew accommodation.

(2)   Whenever possible such ships should also have air conditioning of the radio room and any centralized machinery control room.

2.   The competent authority should –

(a)   investigate the possibility of installing air conditioning in ships of less than 1,000 tons constructed after the adoption of this Recommendation;

(b)   consider the possibility of providing existing ships with air conditioning of all or part of crew accommodation spaces by means of conversion of mechanical ventilation systems to full air conditioning at a time when substantial structural alterations are being made to the accommodation.

3.   The air-conditioning system, whether of a centralized or individual unit type, should be designed –

(a) to maintain the air at a satisfactory temperature and relative humidity as compared to outside air conditions, and to ensure a sufficiency of air changes in all air-conditioned spaces;

(b) to take account of the particular characteristics of operations at sea and not to produce objectionable noises or vibrations.

Crew Accommodation (Noise Control) Recommendation, 1970 (No. 141)

1. (1) The competent authority in each maritime country, in conjunction with the competent international bodies and with representatives of shipowners' and seafarers' organizations, should review research into the problem of noise on board ships with the object of obtaining and pooling data on the basis of which authoritative criteria and standards can be established at an early date, so that national provisions can be drawn up to protect seafarers, so far as necessary, from the ill effects of noise.

(2) Such research should cover –

(a) the effect of exposure to excessive noise on the hearing, health and comfort of seafarers;

(b) the measures which should be prescribed to reduce shipboard noise and/or to protect the hearing of seafarers.

2. The competent authority in each maritime country should, in the light of that research, establish provisions for the reduction of, and protection of seafarers from, excessive and harmful noise on board ship as soon as this becomes reasonably possible.

3. As appropriate in the light of the research, the measures to be considered might include the following:

(a) instruction of seafarers in the dangers to hearing and health of prolonged exposure to high noise levels and in the proper use of noise protection devices and equipment;

(b) provision of ear plugs and/or ear muffs, approved by the competent authority, to seafarers in the engine room where necessary;

(c) the reduction of noise in sleeping rooms, mess rooms, recreation rooms and other crew accommodation by –

    (i) the locating of such spaces as far as practicable from the engines, steering gear rooms, deck winches, ventilation, heating and air-conditioning equipment and other noisy machinery and apparatus;

    (ii) the use of acoustic insulation and other appropriate sound-absorbing materials in the construction and finishing of bulkheads, overheads and decks within the sound-producing spaces, and self-closing noise-isolating doors for machinery spaces;

(d) the reduction and control of noise levels in engine rooms and other machinery spaces by –

(i)   provision, wherever practicable, of soundproof centralized machinery control rooms for engine-room personnel;

(ii)   insulation, as far as practicable, of working spaces such as the machine shop from the general engine-room noise;

(iii)   measures to reduce noise in the operation of machinery.

Prevention of Accidents (Seafarers) Convention, 1970 (No. 134)

Date of entry into force: 17 February 1973

Article 1

1.   For the purpose of this Convention, the term "seafarer" covers all persons who are employed in any capacity on board a ship, other than a ship of war, registered in a territory for which the Convention is in force and ordinarily engaged in maritime navigation.

2.   In the event of any doubt whether any categories of persons are to be regarded as seafarers for the purpose of this Convention, the question shall be determined by the competent authority in each country after consultation with the shipowners, and seafarers' organizations concerned.

3.   For the purpose of this Convention, the term "occupational accidents" covers accidents to seafarers arising out of or in the course of their employment.

Article 2

1.   The competent authority in each maritime country shall take the necessary measures to ensure that occupational accidents are adequately reported and investigated, and comprehensive statistics of such accidents kept and analysed.

2.   All occupational accidents shall be reported and statistics shall not be limited to fatalities or to accidents involving the ship.

3.   The statistics shall record the numbers, nature, causes and effects of occupational accidents, with a clear indication of the department on board ship – for instance, deck, engine or catering – and of the area – for instance, at sea or in port – where the accident occurred.

4.   The competent authority shall undertake an investigation into the causes and circumstances of occupational accidents resulting in loss of life or serious personal injury, and such other accidents as may be specified in national laws or regulations.

Article 3

In order to provide a sound basis for the prevention of accidents which are due to particular hazards of maritime employment, research shall be undertaken into general trends and into such hazards as are brought out by statistics,

Article 4

1.   Provisions concerning the prevention of occupational accidents shall be laid down by laws or regulations, codes of practice or other appropriate means.

2.   These provisions shall refer to any general provisions on the prevention of accidents and the protection of health in employment which may be applicable to the work of seafarers, and shall specify measures for the prevention of accidents which are peculiar to maritime employment.

3.   In particular, these provisions shall cover the following matters:

(a) general and basic provisions;

(b) structural features of the ship;

(c) machinery;

(d) special safety measures on and below deck;

(e) loading and unloading equipment;

(f) fire prevention and fire-fighting;

(g) anchors, chains and lines;

(h) dangerous cargo and ballast;

(i) personal protective equipment for seafarers.

Article 5

1.   The accident prevention provisions referred to in Article 4 shall clearly specify the obligation of shipowners, seafarers and others concerned to comply with them,

2.   Generally, any obligation on the shipowner to provide protective equipment or other accident prevention safeguards shall be accompanied by provision for the use of such equipment and safeguards by seafarers and a requirement that they comply with the relevant accident prevention measures.

Article 6

1.   Appropriate measures shall be taken to ensure the proper application of the provisions referred to in Article 4 by means of adequate inspection or otherwise.

2.   Appropriate measures shall be taken to ensure compliance with these provisions.

3.   All necessary steps shall be taken to ensure that inspection and enforcement authorities are familiar with maritime employment and its practices.

4.   In order to facilitate application, copies or summaries of the provisions shall be brought to the attention of seafarers, for instance by display in a prominent position on board ship.

Article 7

Provision shall be made for the appointment, from amongst the crew of the ship, of a suitable person or suitable persons or of a suitable committee responsible, under the Master, for accident prevention.

Article 8

1.   Programmes for the prevention of occupational accidents shall be established by the competent authority with the cooperation of shipowner and seafarers' organizations.

2.   Implementation of such programmes shall be so organized that the competent authority, shipowners and seafarers or their representatives and other appropriate bodies may play an active part.

3.   In particular, national or local joint accident prevention committees or ad hoc working parties, on which both shipowners' and seafarers' organizations are represented, shall be established.

Article 9

1.   The competent authority shall promote and, in so far as appropriate under national conditions, ensure the inclusion, as part of the instruction in professional duties, of instruction in the prevention of accidents and in measures for the protection of health in employment in the curricula, for all categories and grades of seafarers, of vocational training institutions.

2.   All appropriate and practicable measures shall also be taken to bring to the attention of seafarers information concerning particular hazards, for instance by means of official notices containing relevant instructions.

Article 10

Members, with the assistance as appropriate of intergovernmental and other international organizations, shall endeavour, in cooperation with each other, to achieve the greatest possible measure of uniformity of other action for the prevention of occupational accidents.

Prevention of Accidents (Seafarers) Recommendation, 1970 (No. 142)

1.   For the purpose of this Recommendation –

(a) the term "seafarer" covers all persons who are employed in any capacity on board a ship, other than a ship of war, ordinarily engaged in maritime navigation;

(b) the term "occupational accidents" covers accidents to seafarers arising out of or in the course of their employment.

2.   In giving effect to paragraph 3 of Article 2 of the Prevention of Accidents (Seafarers) Convention, 1970, Members should have due regard to any international system of recording accidents to seafarers which may have been established by the International Labour Organization.

3.   Subjects to be investigated in pursuance of Article 3 of the Prevention of Accidents (Seafarers) Convention, 1970, might include –

(a) working environment, such as working surfaces, layout of machinery and means of access and lighting, and methods of work;

(b) incidence of accidents in different age groups;

(c) special physiological or psychological problems created by the shipboard environment;

(d) problems arising from physical stress on board ship, in particular as a consequence of increased workload;

(e) problems arising from and effects of technical developments and their influence on the composition of crews;

(f) problems arising from any human failures such as carelessness.

4.   In formulating the accident prevention provisions called for by Article 4 of the Prevention of Accidents (Seafarers) Convention, 1970, Members should have due regard to any Code of Practice concerning the safety and health of seafarers which may have been published by the International Labour Office.

5.   In giving effect to Article 5 of the Prevention of Accidents (Seafarers) Convention, 1970, account should be taken of Articles 7 and 11 of the Guarding of Machinery Convention, 1963 – and the corresponding provisions of the Guarding of Machinery Recommendation, 1963 – under which the obligation to ensure compliance with the requirement that machinery in use is properly guarded, and its use without appropriate guards prevented, rests on the employer, while there is an obligation on the worker not to use machinery without the guards being in position nor to make inoperative the guards provided.

6.   (1)   The functions of the committees and other bodies referred to in paragraph 3 of Article 8 of the Prevention of Accidents (Seafarers) Convention, 1970, might include –

(a) the preparation of accident prevention provisions, rules and manuals;

(b) the organization of accident prevention training and programmes;

(c) the organization of accident prevention publicity, including films, posters, notices and brochures;

(d) the distribution of accident prevention literature and information so that it reaches seafarers on board ship.

(2)   Relevant provisions or recommendations adopted by the appropriate national authorities or organizations or responsible international maritime organizations should be taken into account by those preparing texts of accident prevention measures and/or recommended practices.

7.   The syllabuses of the instruction referred to in Article 9 of the Prevention of Accidents (Seafarers) Convention, 1970, should be reviewed periodically and brought up to date in the light of development in types and sizes of ships and in their equipment, as well as changes in crewing practices, nationality, language and the organization of work on board ship.

8.   (1)   There should be continuous accident prevention publicity.

(2)   Such publicity might take the following forms:

(a) instructional films, film strips and shorts, for use in vocational training centres for seafarers and where possible in film programmes screened on board ship;

(b) display of safety posters on board ship;

(c) inclusion of articles on hazards of maritime employment and accident prevention measures in periodicals read by seafarers;

(d) special campaigns, during which various media of publicity are used to instruct seafarers in accident prevention and safe working practices.

(3) The publicity should take into account that there are often seafarers of different nationalities, languages and habits on board ship.

9.   (1) In giving effect to Article 10 of the Accident Prevention (Seafarers) Convention, 1970, Members should have due regard to relevant Model Codes of Safety Regulations or Codes of Practice published by the International Labour Office and the appropriate standards of international organizations for standardization.

(2) Members should further have regard to the need for international cooperation in the continuous promotion of action for the prevention of occupational accidents; such cooperation might take the form of –

(a) bilateral or multilateral arrangements for uniformity in accident prevention standards and safeguards;

(b) exchange of information on particular hazards affecting seafarers and on means of preventing accidents;

(c) assistance in testing of equipment and inspection according to the national regulations of the country of registration of the ship;

(d) collaboration in the preparation and dissemination of accident prevention provisions, rules or manuals;

(e) collaboration in the production and use of training aids;

(f) joint facilities for or mutual assistance in the training of seafarers in accident prevention and safe working practices.

Seamen's Welfare in Ports Recommendation, 1936 (No. 48)

Whereas by the nature of their calling seamen are frequently deprived for long periods of the advantages of family life and may be exposed while in ports, particularly in foreign countries, to special dangers and difficulties and whereas it is not always possible for them to have the benefit of arrangements made to organize the spare time, promote the welfare and safeguard the health of the general body of workers,

Whereas certain Governments and different private associations have successfully taken various measures for the special help and protection of seamen in ports and whereas such protection should be extended to as large a number of seamen as possible, and

Whereas it is important, notwithstanding differences which may exist in national and local needs and customs, to develop and coordinate nationally and internationally the principal forms of action, in a manner which draws no distinction of race between seamen;

The Conference recommends that each Member of the International Labour Organization should take the following principles and methods into consideration for the promotion of the welfare of both national and foreign seamen in ports.

PART I. GENERAL ORGANIZATION

1.   It is desirable to create in every important port an official or officially recognized body, which might comprise representatives of shipowners, seamen, national and local authorities and the chief associations concerned, for the purposes of –

(a) collecting, as far as possible in conjunction with the different authorities or organizations concerned, including the consular authorities of maritime States, all useful information and suggestions on the conditions for seamen in the port;

(b) advising the competent departments, authorities and associations as to the adoption, adaptation and coordination of measures for the improvement of such conditions; and

(c) collaborating if required with other competent bodies in carrying out such measures.

2.   It is desirable, in order to enable the International Labour Office to inform the Governments of the maritime States and to assist them to coordinate their action, that each of them should keep in touch with the Office and furnish it every three years with all useful information on the experience acquired in the promotion of seamen's welfare in ports and on the progress made in this field.

PART II. REGULATION

3.   There should be laws or regulations to protect seamen, by measures including the following, from the dangers to which they are exposed in certain establishments or in the docks as such:

(a) the regulation of the sale of intoxicating liquor;

(b) the prohibition of the employment in public houses of young persons of either sex under a certain age;

(c) the application of the provisions of international agreements limiting the sale and use of narcotics to all seamen without distinction of nationality;

(d) the prohibition of the entry into the docks and harbour area generally of undesirable persons;

(e) the fencing off of dock areas and the protection of the edges of wharves and quays and other dangerous parts of docks by fixed or movable barriers, wherever such measures are practicable;

(f) the provision of sufficient lighting and, where necessary, of signposts for docks and approaches.

4.   In order to ensure the strict enforcement of the measures indicated above and to increase their efficacy, there should be arrangements for supervision, including –

(a) supervision of establishments where intoxicating liquors are sold and, where necessary and practicable, of hotels, cafés, lodging houses and other similar establishments in the harbour area;

(b) supervision, which might be carried out jointly by masters and the public authorities, of persons visiting ships, including boatmen plying between ships and the shore, with a view to preventing intoxicating liquor or narcotics being wrongfully brought on board or the fulfilment of any other illicit purpose;

(c) the maintenance in the harbour area of adequate police forces, specially trained and equipped, which should keep in touch with the other supervising bodies.

5. For the better protection of foreign seamen, measures should be taken to facilitate –

(a) their relations with their consuls; and

(b) effective cooperation between consuls and the local or national authorities.

PART III. HEALTH

6. Soliciting and enticing, whether directly or indirectly, in the neighbourhood of the harbour and in districts frequented by seamen should be energetically repressed.

7. All suitable measures should be taken to make known to seamen entering the port, irrespective of their nationality –

(a) the dangers and means of preventing diseases to which they are exposed, including more particularly tuberculosis and tropical and venereal diseases;

(b) the necessity for persons suffering from disease to undergo treatment and the facilities available for such treatment; and

(c) the dangers arising from the habit of using narcotics.

8. The treatment of seamen suffering from disease should be facilitated by suitable measures including –

(a) as wide extension as possible, especially in the dock area, of free and continued treatment for venereal diseases, as provided for example by the Agreement concerning Facilities to be given to Merchant Seamen for the Treatment of Venereal Diseases, signed at Brussels, 1 December 1924;

(b) the admission of seamen to clinics and hospitals in ports, without difficulty and irrespective of nationality or religious belief;

(c) as wide application as possible to foreign seamen of the provision made for the protection of nationals against tuberculosis;

(d) the provision, whenever possible, of arrangements, designed to ensure, when necessary, continuation of treatment with a view to supplementing the medical facilities available to seamen.

PART IV. ACCOMMODATION AND RECREATION

9. Arrangements should be made, at least in the larger ports, for the material and general assistance of seamen while in the port and such arrangements should more particularly include –

(a) the institution or development of seamen's hostels of a satisfactory character and furnishing suitable board and lodging at reasonable prices;

(b) the institution or development of institutes – which might be distinct from the seamen's hostels, but should keep as far as possible in touch with them – providing meeting and recreation rooms (canteens, rooms for games, libraries, etc.);

(c) the organization, where possible in cooperation with ships' sports clubs, of healthy recreations, such as sports, excursions, etc.;

(d) the promotion, by every possible means, of the family life of seamen.

PART V. SAVINGS AND REMITTANCE OF WAGES

10. In order to help seamen to save and to transmit their savings to their families –

(a) there should be adopted a simple, rapid and safe system, operating with the assistance of consuls, masters, shipowners' agents or reliable private institutions for enabling seamen, and more especially those who are in a foreign country, to deposit or remit the whole or part of their wages;

(b) a system for enabling seamen, at the time of their signing on or during the voyage, to allot, if they so desire, a proportion of their wages for remittance at regular intervals to their families should be instituted or made of more general application.

PART VI. INFORMATION FOR SEAMEN

11. In view of the fact that the success of most of the measures recommended above must depend to a large extent on suitable publicity among seamen, such publicity should be organized and undertaken by the public authorities, the bodies referred to in Part I of this Recommendation, and the competent associations, assisted as far as possible by the ship's officers and doctor and by ships' sports clubs.

12. Such publicity might include –

(a) the distribution on shore and, subject to the consent of the master, on board ship, of pamphlets in the most appropriate languages giving clear information as to the facilities available for seamen in the port of call or in the next ports for which the ship is bound;

(b) the creation in the larger ports of information offices, either at shipping offices or elsewhere, easily accessible to seamen and staffed by persons capable of giving directly such explanations or guidance as may be useful;

(c) the inclusion of some useful information for the physical well-being and general protection of seamen in seamen's books, discharge books or other documents habitually carried by seamen, or in notices posted in a conspicuous place in the crew's quarters;

(d) the frequent publication of articles of general and educational interest to seamen in periodicals read by seamen, both of specialized and general interest, and also the use of the cinema for this purpose;

(e) the distribution of information concerning the tariffs of local transport and of local places of interest and entertainment.

PART VII. EQUALITY OF TREATMENT

13. Governments, authorities and organizations which may have to administer funds for the welfare of seamen are specially urged not to concern themselves solely with seamen of a particular nationality, but to act as generously as possible in the spirit of international solidarity.

Seafarers' Welfare Recommendation, 1970 (No. 138)

I. ORGANIZATION AND FINANCING OF WELFARE ACTIVITIES

1. Welfare schemes should be systematically organized and financing should be on an adequate and regular basis.

2. Welfare services should be reviewed frequently to ensure that they keep pace with changes in the needs of seafarers resulting from technical, operational and other developments in the shipping industry.

3. There should be national, regional and/or port welfare boards, on which representative shipowners' and seafarers' organizations, the competent authorities and, where desirable and appropriate, voluntary organizations and social bodies concerned should be represented.

4. The functions of such boards should include surveying the need for, and assisting and coordinating, welfare facilities in the area for which the board is responsible.

5. Consuls and local representatives of foreign welfare organizations should, as appropriate, be associated with the work of regional and port welfare boards.

6. Measures should be taken to ensure that, as necessary, technically competent persons are employed full time in the operation of seafarers' welfare facilities, in addition to voluntary workers.

7. Where large numbers of seafarers of different nationalities require facilities such as hotels, clubs and sports facilities in a particular port, the competent authorities or bodies of the countries of origin of the seafarers and of the flag States should consult and cooperate with the competent authorities and bodies of the country in which the port is situated and with each other, with a view both to the pooling of resources and to avoiding unnecessary duplication.

8. With a view to better organizing welfare and leisure activities and stimulating the use of welfare materials on board ship, instruction in the organization of welfare activities on board should be included in training courses for officers

and ratings. Consideration should be given to the periodic assignment to merchant vessels of an officer specially trained in such work.

II. ACCOMMODATION IN PORTS

9.   Seafarers' hotels or hostels should be maintained in all ports of interest to international shipping where there is a need for them; they should provide facilities equal to those found in a good class hotel, and should wherever possible be located in good surroundings away from the immediate vicinity of the docks.

10.   These accommodation facilities should be open to seafarers of all nationalities, irrespective of colour, race or creed. Without in any way infringing this principle, it may be necessary in certain ports to provide several types of facilities, comparable in standard but adapted to the customs and needs of different groups of seafarers,

11.   Where necessary and possible, provision should be made for accommodating seafarers' families in seafarers' hotels and hostels.

12.   Prices charged for board and accommodation in seafarers' hotels and hostels should be kept at a reasonable level.

13.   Seafarers' hotels and hostels should be properly supervised on the same basis as other comparable establishments.

III. GENERAL WELFARE MEASURES IN PORT AND ON BOARD SHIP

14.   Governments should take measures designed to overcome restrictions on and to expedite the free circulation among ships, central supply agencies and welfare establishments of welfare materials such as films, books, newspapers and sports equipment for use by seafarers on board their ships and in welfare centres ashore.

15.   Every effort should be made to ensure that the forwarding of seafarers' mail is as reliable and expeditious as possible. Efforts should be made also to avoid seafarers being required to pay additional postage when mail has to be readdressed owing to circumstances beyond their control.

16.   Adequate means of transportation at moderate prices should be available at any reasonable time when needed in order to enable seafarers to reach city centres from port areas.

17.   Every effort should be made by those responsible to facilitate the granting of shore leave to officers and ratings as soon as possible after a ship's arrival in port.

18.   In order to ensure the maintenance of seafarers' family ties in the special conditions of their employment, the granting of leave at home at reasonable intervals should be encouraged.

19.   Measures should be taken to ensure, subject to any national or international laws or regulations, that whenever possible and reasonable both officers and

ratings are expeditiously granted permission to have their wives, other relatives and friends as visitors on board their ships when in port.

20. Consideration should be given to the possibility of allowing the wives of seafarers to accompany their husbands on an occasional voyage, where this is practicable and reasonable. Wives who so accompany their husbands should carry adequate insurance cover against accident and illness; the shipowner should give every assistance to the seafarer to effect such insurance.

21. Where possible and appropriate, the provision of canteens on board ship for officers and ratings should be considered, unless this is contrary to national, religious or social customs.

22. Where possible, consideration should be given to the provision on board ship of facilities for the projection of films, television viewing, handicrafts and reading.

IV. RECREATION FACILITIES IN PORT AND ON BOARD SHIP

23. Centres providing meeting and recreation rooms for seafarers of all nationalities should be established or developed in all ports of interest to international shipping where there is a need for them.

24. Healthy recreation such as hobbies, gymnastics, games or sports, both ashore and on board, as well as excursions to places of interest, should be encouraged and should be organized by and for seafarers with assistance as appropriate from the port welfare bodies. Where possible, facilities for swimming should be provided on board ship,

25. All seafarers visiting a port should, where practicable and possible, have the opportunity of taking part in sports and outdoor recreation; for this purpose suitable facilities should be made available, for example by providing sports fields for the use of seafarers or by arranging for them access to existing sports fields.

26. There should be cooperation among the competent authorities of different countries, shipowners' and seafarers' organizations, welfare organizations and ships' captains in the establishment of international seafarers' sports competitions such as lifeboat races, athletics and football matches.

V. INFORMATION AND EDUCATIONAL FACILITIES IN PORT AND ON BOARD SHIP

27. Appropriate vocational training schemes for seafarers should include education and information on matters affecting their welfare, including general health hazards.

28. Information should be disseminated among seafarers concerning facilities open to the general public in ports of call – particularly transport, welfare and educational facilities and places of worship – as well as facilities provided specially for seafarers. Such information could be in the form of a booklet, printed in several languages, which also contains a plan of the city and port.

29.   Interesting and culturally profitable spare-time activities on board ship should be encouraged through the supply of suitable literature and assistance in pursuing hobby activities and amateur entertainment.

30.   Correspondence courses in a variety of subjects of interest to seafarers should be available; other educational aids, such as film projectors, film library services and a tape recorder, should be provided on individual ships where appropriate.

Seafarers' Welfare Convention, 1987 (No. 163)
Date of entry into force: 3 October 1990
Article I

1.   For the purposes of this Convention –

(a)   the term "seafarer" means any person who is employed in any capacity on board a seagoing ship, whether publicly or privately owned, other than a ship of war;

(b)   the term "welfare facilities and services" means welfare, cultural, recreational and information facilities and services.

2.   Each Member shall determine by national laws or regulations, after consultation with the representative organizations of shipowners and seafarers, which ships registered in its territory are to be regarded as seagoing ships for the purpose of the provisions of this Convention relating to welfare facilities and services on board ship.

3.   To the extent it deems practicable, after consultation with the representative organizations of fishing vessel owners and fishermen, the competent authority shall apply the provisions of this Convention to commercial maritime fishing.

Article 2

1.   Each Member for which this Convention is in force undertakes to ensure that adequate welfare facilities and services are provided for seafarers both in port and on board ship.

2.   Each Member shall ensure that the necessary arrangements are made for financing the welfare facilities and services provided in accordance with the provisions of this Convention.

Article 3

1.   Each Member undertakes to ensure that welfare facilities and services are provided in appropriate ports of the country for all seafarers, irrespective of nationality, race, colour, sex, religion, political opinion or social origin and irrespective of the State in which the ship on which they are employed is registered.

2.   Each Member shall determine, after consultation with the representative organizations of shipowners and seafarers, which ports are to be regarded as appropriate for the purposes of this Article.

Article 4

Each Member undertakes to ensure that the welfare facilities and services on every seagoing ship, whether publicly or privately owned, which is registered in its territory, are provided for the benefit of all seafarers on board.

Article 5

Welfare facilities and services shall be reviewed frequently to ensure that they are appropriate in the light of changes in the needs of seafarers resulting from technical, operational and other developments in the shipping industry.

Article 6

Each Member undertakes –

(a) to cooperate with other Members with a view to ensuring the application of this Convention; and

(b) to ensure cooperation between the parties engaged and interested in promoting the welfare of seafarers at sea and in port.

Seafarers' Welfare Recommendation, 1987 (No. 173)

I. GENERAL

1. For the purposes of this Recommendation –

(a) the term "seafarer" means any person who is employed in any capacity on board a seagoing ship, whether publicly or privately owned, other than a ship of war;

(b) the term "welfare facilities and services" means welfare, cultural, recreational and information facilities and services.

2. To the extent it deems practicable, after consultation with the representative organizations of fishing vessel owners and fishermen, the competent authority should apply the provisions of this Recommendation to commercial maritime fishing.

3. (1) Measures should be taken by Members to ensure that adequate welfare facilities and services are provided for seafarers both in port and on board ship, and that adequate protection is provided to seafarers in the exercise of their calling.

(2) In the implementation of these measures, Members should take into account the special needs of seafarers, especially when in foreign countries and when entering war zones, in respect of their safety, health and spare-time activities.

4. Arrangements for the supervision of welfare facilities and services should include participation by representative organizations of seafarers and shipowners.

5. The welfare facilities and services provided pursuant to this Recommendation should be available to all seafarers, irrespective of nationality, race,

colour, sex, religion, political opinion or social origin and irrespective of the State in which the ship on which they are employed is registered.

6. Members should cooperate with one another in promoting the welfare of seafarers at sea and in port. Such cooperation should included the following:

(a) consultations between the competent authorities aimed at the provision and improvement of seafarers' welfare facilities and services, both in port and on board ship;

(b) agreements on the pooling of resources and the joint provision of welfare facilities in major ports so as to avoid unnecessary duplication;

(c) organizing international sports competitions and encouraging the participation of seafarers in sports activities;

(d) organizing international seminars on the subject of welfare of seafarers at sea and in port.

II. WELFARE FACILITIES AND SERVICES IN PORTS

7. (1) Members should provide or ensure the provision of such welfare facilities and services as may be required in appropriate ports of the country.

(2) Members should consult with the representative organizations of shipowners and seafarers in determining the appropriate ports.

(3) Welfare facilities and services should be reviewed frequently to ensure that they are appropriate in the light of changes in the needs of seafarers resulting from technical, operational and other developments in the shipping industry.

8. (1) Welfare facilities and services should be provided, in accordance with national conditions and practice, by one or more of the following:

(a) the public authorities;

(b) the shipowners' and seafarers' organizations under collective agreements or other agreed arrangements;

(c) voluntary organizations.

(2) Measures should be taken to ensure that, as necessary, technically competent persons are employed full-time in the operation of seafarers' welfare facilities and services, in addition to any voluntary workers.

9. (1) Welfare boards should be established, at the port, regional and national levels, as appropriate, whose functions should include –

(a) keeping under review the adequacy of existing welfare facilities and monitoring the need for the provision of additional facilities or the withdrawal of underutilized facilities;

(b) assisting and advising those responsible for providing welfare facilities and ensuring coordination between them.

(2) Welfare boards should include among their members representatives of organizations of shipowners and seafarers, the competent authorities and, where appropriate, voluntary organizations and social bodies.

(3)   As appropriate, consuls of maritime States and local representatives of foreign welfare organizations should be associated with the work of port, regional and national welfare boards in accordance with national laws and regulations.

10.   (1)   Members should ensure that adequate and regular financial support is provided for seafarers' welfare facilities and services.

(2)   In accordance with national conditions and practice, this financial support should be made available through one or more of the following:

(a)   grants from public funds;

(b)   levies or other special dues from shipping sources;

(c)   voluntary contributions from shipowners, seafarers, or their organizations;

(d)   voluntary contributions from other sources.

(3)   Where welfare taxes, levies and special dues are imposed, they should be used only for the purposes for which they are raised.

11.   Hotels or hostels suitable for seafarers should be available where there is need for them. Such hotels or hostels should be properly supervised, the prices charged should be reasonable in amount and, where necessary and possible, provision should be made for accommodating seafarers' families.

12.   (1)   Necessary welfare and recreational facilities should be established or developed in ports. These should include –

(a)   meeting and recreation rooms as required;

(b)   facilities for sports and outdoor facilities, including competitions;

(c)   educational facilities;

(d)   where appropriate, facilities for religious observances and for personal counselling.

(2)   These facilities may be provided by making available to seafarers in accordance with their needs facilities designed for more general use.

13.   Where large numbers of seafarers of different nationalities require facilities such as hotels, clubs and sports facilities in a particular port, the competent authorities or bodies of the countries of origin of the seafarers and of the flag States, as well as the international associations concerned, should consult and cooperate with the competent authorities and bodies of the country in which the port is situated and with one another, with a view to the pooling of resources and to avoiding unnecessary duplication.

14.   (1)   Information should be disseminated among seafarers concerning facilities open to the general public in ports of call – particularly transport, welfare, entertainment and educational facilities and places of worship – as well as facilities provided specifically for seafarers.

(2)   The means of disseminating such information might include –

(a)   the distribution on shore and, subject to the consent of the master, on board ship, of booklets in the most appropriate languages giving clear information as to the facilities available for seafarers in the port of call or in the next port for which the ship is bound; such booklets should contain a plan of the urban area and port;

(b) the creation in the larger ports of information offices, easily accessible to seafarers and staffed by persons capable of giving directly such explanations and guidance as may be useful.

15.   Adequate means of transportation at moderate prices should be available at any reasonable time, when needed in order to enable seafarers to reach urban areas from convenient locations in the port.

16.   All suitable measures should be taken to make known to seafarers entering port –

(a)   any particular hazards and diseases to which they may be exposed and means of avoiding them;

(b)   the necessity for persons suffering from diseases to undergo early treatment and the nearest facilities available for such treatment;

(c)   the dangers arising from the use of narcotics and alcohol.

17.   Measures should be taken to ensure that seafarers have access when in port to –

(a)   out-patient treatment for sickness and injury;

(b)   hospitalization when necessary;

(c)   facilities for dental treatment, especially in cases of emergency.

18.   All suitable measures should be taken by the competent authorities to make known to shipowners and to seafarers entering port any special laws and customs, the contravention of which may jeopardize their freedom.

19.   Port areas and access roads should be provided by the competent authorities with adequate lighting and signposting and regular patrols for the protection of seafarers.

20.   (1)   For the protection of foreign seafarers, measures should be taken to facilitate –

(a)   access to their consuls;

(b)   effective cooperation between consuls and the local or national authorities.

(2)   Whenever a seafarer is detained for any reason in the territory of a Member, the competent authority should, if he so requests, immediately inform the flag State and the State of nationality of the seafarer. The competent authority should promptly inform the seafarer of the right to make such a request. The State of nationality of the seafarer should promptly notify the seafarer's next of kin. If a seafarer is interned, the Member should allow consular officers of these States immediate access to the seafarer and regular visits thereafter so long as the seafarer is interned.

(3)   The case of a detained seafarer should be dealt with promptly under due process of law, and the flag State and the State of nationality of the detained seafarer should be kept informed of developments as they occur.

21. (1) Every possible practical assistance should be given to seafarers stranded in foreign ports pending their repatriation.

(2) In the event of delay in the repatriation of seafarers, the competent authority should ensure that the consular or local representative of the flag State is informed immediately.

22. Members should take measures, whenever necessary, to ensure the safety of seafarers from aggression and other unlawful acts while ships are in their territorial waters and especially in approaches to ports.

III. WELFARE FACILITIES AND SERVICES AT SEA

23. (1) Welfare facilities and amenities should be provided on board ship for the benefit of the seafarers. Where practicable such facilities should include –

(a) television viewing and the reception of radio broadcasts;

(b) projection of films or video films, the stock of which should be adequate for the duration of the voyage and, where necessary, changed at reasonable intervals;

(c) sports equipment including exercise equipment, table games, deck games;

(d) where possible, facilities for swimming;

(e) a library containing vocational and other books, the stock of which should be adequate for the duration of the voyage and changed at reasonable intervals;

(f) facilities for recreational handicrafts.

(2) Where possible and appropriate, the provision of bars on board ship for seafarers should be considered, unless this is contrary to national, religious or social customs.

24. Vocational training schemes for seafarers should, where appropriate, include education and information on matters affecting their welfare, including general health hazards.

25. (1) Access to ship-to-shore telephone communications, where available, should be granted and charges for the use of the service should be reasonable in amount.

(2) Every effort should be made to ensure that the forwarding of seafarers' mail is as reliable and expeditious as possible. Efforts should also be made to avoid seafarers being required to pay additional postage when mail has to be readdressed owing to circumstances beyond their control.

26. (1) Measures should be taken to ensure, subject to any applicable national or international laws or regulations, that whenever possible and reasonable seafarers are expeditiously granted permission to have their spouses, relatives and friends as visitors on board their ship when in port.

(2) Consideration should be given to the possibility of allowing seafarers to be accompanied by their spouses on an occasional voyage where this is practicable and reasonable. Such spouses should carry adequate insurance cover against

accident and illness; the shipowners should give every assistance to the seafarer to effect such insurance.

27.   Every effort should be made by those responsible in port and on board ship to facilitate shore leave for seafarers as soon as possible after a ship's arrival in port.

IV.   SAVINGS AND REMITTANCE OF WAGES

28.   In order to help seafarers to save and to transmit their savings to their families –

(a)   there should be adopted a simple, rapid and safe system, operating with the assistance of consuls or other competent authorities, masters, shipowners' agents or reliable financial institutions, for enabling seafarers, and more especially those who are in a foreign country or serving in a ship registered in a country other than their own, to deposit or remit the whole or part of their wages;

(b)   a system for enabling seafarers, at the time of their signing on or during the voyage, to allot, if they so desire, a proportion of their wages for remittance at regular intervals to their families should be instituted or made of more general application;

(c)   allotments should be remitted in due time and directly to the person or persons nominated by the seafarers;

(d)   efforts should be made to provide independent confirmation that seafarers' allotments are actually remitted to the person or persons nominated.

Health Protection and Medical Care (Seafarers) Convention, 1987 (No. 164)

Date of entry into force: 11 January 1991

Article 1

1.   This Convention applies to every seagoing ship whether publicly or privately owned, which is registered in the territory of any Member for which the Convention is in force and which is ordinarily engaged in commercial maritime navigation.

2.   To the extent it deems practicable, after consultation with the representative organizations of fishing vessel owners and fishermen, the competent authority shall apply the provisions of this Convention to commercial maritime fishing.

3.   In the event of doubt as to whether or not any ships are to be regarded as engaged in commercial maritime navigation or commercial maritime fishing for the purpose of this Convention, the question shall be determined by the competent authority after consultation with the organizations of shipowners, seafarers and fishermen concerned.

4.   For the purpose of this Convention the term "seafarer" means any person who is employed in any capacity on board a seagoing ship to which this Convention applies.

Article 2

Effect shall be given to this Convention by national laws or regulations, collective agreements, works rules, arbitration awards or court decisions or other means appropriate to national conditions.

Article 3

Each Member shall by national laws or regulations make shipowners responsible for keeping ships in proper sanitary and hygienic conditions.

Article 4

Each Member shall ensure that measures providing for health protection and medical care for seafarers on board ship are adopted which –

(a) ensure the application to seafarers of any general provisions on occupational health protection and medical care relevant to the seafaring profession, as well as of special provisions peculiar to work on board;

(b) aim at providing seafarers with health protection and medical care as comparable as possible to that which is generally available to workers ashore;

(c) guarantee seafarers the right to visit a doctor without delay in ports of call where practicable;

(d) ensure that, in accordance with national law and practice, medical care and health protection while a seafarer is serving on articles are provided free of charge to seafarers;

(e) are not limited to treatment of sick or injured seafarers but include measures of a preventive character, and devote particular attention to the development of health promotion and health education programmes in order that seafarers themselves may play an active part in reducing the incidence of ill-health among their number.

Article 5

1. Every ship to which this Convention applies shall be required to carry a medicine chest.

2. The contents of the medicine chest and the medical equipment carried on board shall be prescribed by the competent authority taking into account such factors as the type of ship, the number of persons on board and the nature, destination and duration of voyages.

3. In adopting or reviewing the national provisions concerning the contents of the medicine chest and the medical equipment carried on board, the competent authority shall take into account international recommendations in this field, such as the most recent edition of the *International medical guide for ships* and the *List of essential drugs* published by the World Health Organization, as well as advances in medical knowledge and approved methods of treatment.

4. The medicine chest and its contents as well as the medical equipment carried on board shall be properly maintained and inspected at regular intervals, not exceeding 12 months, by responsible persons designated by the competent

authority, who shall ensure that the expiry dates and conditions of storage of all medicines are checked.

5.   The competent authority shall ensure that the contents of the medicine chest are listed and labelled with generic names in addition to any brand names used, expiry dates and conditions of storage, and that they conform to the medical guide used nationally.

6.   The competent authority shall ensure that where a cargo which is classified dangerous has not been included in the most recent edition of the *Medical first aid guide for use in accidents involving dangerous goods* published by the International Maritime Organization, the necessary information on the nature of the substances, the risks involved, the necessary personal protective devices, the relevant medical procedures and specific antidotes is made available to the master, seafarers and other interested persons. Such specific antidotes and personal protective devices shall be on board whenever dangerous goods are carried.

7.   In cases of urgent necessity and when a medicine prescribed by qualified medical personnel for a seafarer is not available in the medicine chest, the shipowner shall take all necessary steps to obtain it as soon as possible.

Article 6

1.   Every ship to which this Convention applies shall be required to carry a ship's medical guide adopted by the competent authority.

2.   The medical guide shall explain how the contents of the medicine chest are to be used and shall be designed to enable persons other than a doctor to care for the sick or injured on board both with and without medical advice by radio or satellite communication.

3.   In adopting or reviewing the ship's medical guide used nationally, the competent authority shall take into account international recommendations in this field, including the most recent edition of the *International medical guide for ships* and the *Medical first aid guide for use in accidents involving dangerous goods*.

Article 7

1.   The competent authority shall ensure by a prearranged system that medical advice by radio or satellite communication to ships at sea, including specialist advice, is available at any hour of the day or night.

2.   Such medical advice, including the onward transmission of medical messages by radio or satellite communication between a ship and those ashore giving the advice, shall be available free of charge to all ships irrespective of the territory in which they are registered.

3.   With a view to ensuring that optimum use is made of facilities available for medical advice by radio or satellite communication –

(a)   all ships to which this Convention applies which are equipped with radio installations shall carry a complete list of radio stations through which medical advice can be obtained;

(b) all ships to which this Convention applies which are equipped with a system of satellite communication shall carry a complete list of coast earth stations through which medical advice can be obtained;

(c) the lists shall be kept up to date and in the custody of the person on board responsible for communication duties.

4. Seafarers on board requesting medical advice by radio or satellite communication shall be instructed in the use of the ship's medical guide and the medical section of the most recent edition of the *International code of signals* published by the International Maritime Organization so as to enable them to understand the type of information needed by the advising doctor as well as the advice received.

5. The competent authority shall ensure that doctors providing medical advice in accordance with this Article receive appropriate training and are aware of shipboard conditions.

Article 8

1. All ships to which this Convention applies carrying 100 or more seafarers and ordinarily engaged on international voyages of more then three days' duration shall carry a medical doctor as a member of the crew responsible for providing medical care.

2. National laws or regulations shall determine which other ships shall be required to carry a medical doctor as a member of the crew, taking into account, inter alia, such factors as the duration, nature and conditions of the voyage and the number of seafarers on board.

Article 9

1. All ships to which this Convention applies and which do not carry a doctor shall carry as members of the crew one or more specified persons in charge of medical care and the administering of medicines as part of their regular duties.

2. Persons in charge of medical care on board who are not doctors shall have satisfactorily completed a course approved by the competent authority of theoretical and applied training in medical skills. This course shall comprise –

(a) for ships of less than 1,600 gross tonnage which ordinarily are capable of reaching qualified medical care and medical facilities within eight hours, elementary training which will enable such persons to take immediate, effective action in case of accidents or illnesses likely to occur on board ship and to make use of medical advice by radio or satellite communication;

(b) for all other ships, more advanced medical training, including practical training in the emergency/casualty department of a hospital where practicable and training in life-saving techniques such as intravenous therapy, which will enable the persons concerned to participate effectively in coordinated schemes for medical assistance to ships at sea, and to provide the sick or injured with a satisfactory standard of medical care during the period they are likely to remain on board. Wherever possible, this training shall be provided under the supervision of a physician with a thorough knowledge and understanding of the medical problems and circumstances relating to the seafaring profession, including expert knowledge of radio or satellite communication medical services.

3.   The courses referred to in this Article shall be based on the contents of the most recent edition of the *International medical guide for ships*, the *Medical first aid guide for use in accidents involving dangerous goods*, the *Document for guidance – An international maritime training guide* published by the International Maritime Organization, and the medical section of the *International code of signals* as well as similar national guides.

4.   Persons referred to in paragraph 2 of this Article and such other seafarers as may be required by the competent authority shall undergo refresher courses to enable them to maintain and increase their knowledge and skills and to keep abreast of new developments, at approximately five-year intervals.

5.   All seafarers, during their maritime vocational training, shall receive instruction on the immediate action that should be taken on encountering an accident or other medical emergency on board.

6.   In addition to the person or persons in charge of medical care on board, a specified crew member or crew members shall receive elementary training in medical care to enable him or them to take immediate effective action in case of accidents or illnesses likely to occur on board ship.

Article 10

All ships to which this Convention applies shall provide all possible medical assistance, where practicable, to other vessels which may request it.

Article 11

1.   In any ship of 500 or more gross tonnage, carrying 15 or more seafarers and engaged in a voyage of more than three days' duration, separate hospital accommodation shall be provided. The competent authority may relax this requirement in respect of ships engaged in coastal trade.

2.   In any ship of between 200 and 500 gross tonnage and in tugs this Article shall be applied where reasonable and practicable.

3.   This Article does not apply to ships primarily propelled by sail.

4.   The hospital accommodation shall be suitably situated, so that it is easy of access and so that the occupants may be comfortably housed and may receive proper attention in all weathers.

5.   The hospital accommodation shall be so designed as to facilitate consultation and the giving of medical first aid.

6.   The arrangement of the entrance, berths, lighting, ventilation, heating and water supply shall be designed to ensure the comfort and facilitate the treatment of the occupants.

7.   The number of hospital berths required shall be prescribed by the competent authority.

8. Water closet accommodation shall be provided for the exclusive use of the occupants of the hospital accommodation, either as part of the accommodation or in close proximity thereto.

9. Hospital accommodation shall not be used for other than medical purposes.

Article 12

1. A standard medical report form for seafarers shall be adopted by the competent authority as a model for use by ships' doctors, masters or persons in charge of medical care on board and hospitals or doctors ashore.

2. The form shall be specially designed to facilitate the exchange of medical and related information concerning individual seafarers between ship and shore in cases of illness or injury.

3. The information contained in the medical report form shall be kept confidential and shall be used for no other purpose than to facilitate the treatment of seafarers.

Article 13

1. Members for which this Convention is in force shall cooperate with one another in promoting protection of the health of seafarers and medical care for them on board ship.

2. Such cooperation might cover the following matters:

(a) developing and coordinating search and rescue efforts and arranging prompt medical help and evacuation at sea for the seriously ill or injured on board a ship through such means as periodic ship position reporting systems, rescue coordination centres and emergency helicopter services, in conformity with the provisions of the International Convention of Maritime Search and Rescue, 1979, and the *Merchant ship search and rescue manual* and *IMO search and rescue manual* developed by the International Maritime Organization;

(b) making optimum use of fishing vessels carrying a doctor and stationing ships at sea which can provide hospital and rescue facilities;

(c) compiling and maintaining an international list of doctors and medical care facilities available worldwide to provide emergency medical care to seafarers;

(d) landing seafarers in port for emergency treatment;

(e) repatriating seafarers hospitalized abroad as soon as practicable, in accordance with the medical advice of the doctors responsible for the case, which takes into account the seafarer's wishes and needs;

(f) arranging personal assistance for seafarers during repatriation, in accordance with the medical advice of the doctors responsible for the case, which takes into account the seafarer's wishes and needs;

(g) endeavouring to set up health centres for seafarers to –

(i) conduct research on the health status, medical treatment and preventive health care of seafarers;

(ii) train medical and health service staff in maritime medicine;

(h) collecting and evaluating statistics concerning occupational accidents, diseases and fatalities to seafarers and integrating and harmonizing them with any existing national system of statistics on occupational accidents, diseases and fatalities covering other categories of workers;

(i) organizing international exchanges of technical information, training material and personnel, as well as international training courses, seminars and working groups, providing all seafarers with special curative and preventive health and medical services in port, or making available to them general health, medical and rehabilitation services;

(k) arranging for the repatriation of the bodies or ashes, in accordance with the wishes of the next of kin, of deceased seafarers as soon as practicable.

3.   International cooperation in the field of health protection and medical care for seafarers shall be based on bilateral or multilateral agreements or consultations among Members.

Ships' Medicine Chests Recommendation, 1958 (No. 105)

The Conference recommends that each Member should apply the following provisions:

1.   (1)   Every vessel engaged in maritime navigation should be required to carry a medicine chest, the contents of which should be prescribed by the competent authority, taking into account such factors as the number of persons on board, and the nature and the duration of the voyage. Special provision should be made for the custody, by the master or other responsible officer, of medicaments the use of which is restricted.

(2)   The rules and regulations concerning the minimum contents of the medicine chests should apply whether there is a ship's doctor on board or not.

2.   (1)   In establishing or reviewing rules or regulations concerning the contents of the various types of medicine chests, the competent authority should take into consideration the list of minimum contents appended to this Recommendation.

(2)   Such rules or regulations should be subject to periodical revision in the light of new medical discoveries, advances and approved methods of treatment, in accordance with any proposals for such revision which may be adopted in a manner agreed between the International Labour Organization and the World Health Organization.

3.   All medicine chests should contain a medical guide approved by the competent authority, which explains fully how the contents of the medicine chest are to be used. The guide should be sufficiently detailed to enable persons other

than a ship's doctor to administer to the needs of sick or injured persons on board both with and without supplementary medical advice by radio.

4. The rules and regulations should provide for the proper maintenance and care of medicine chests and their contents and their regular inspection at intervals not normally exceeding 12 months by persons authorized by the competent authority.

Annex

Minimum list of medicaments and medical equipment[1]

A. *Medicaments corresponding to the following preparations described in the* International Pharmacopoeia

(a)   In Volume I:

   * Antidiphtheria serum.
   * Antitetanus serum (small quantities).
   Ethanolic solution of iodine.
   Tincture of opium (and/or equivalent).

(b)   In Volume II:

   * Injection of adrenalin.
   * Injection of atropine sulfate.
   Injection of morphine.
   * Injection of nikethamide.
   * Injection of procaine hydrochloride.
   Tablets of acetylsalicylic acid.
   * Tablets of ascorbic acid.
   * Tablets of amphetamine sulfate.
   Tablets of codeine phosphate (and/or equivalent).
   Tablets of ephedrine hydrochloride.
   * Tablets of glyceryl trinitrate.
   * Tablets of mercurous chloride (calomel).
   * Tablets of proguanil hydrochloride (and/or other anti-malarial drug).
   Tablets of succinylsulfathiazole (or equivalent).
   Tablets of sulfadiazine (or equivalent).
   * Tincture of belladonna.
   Water for injection.

B. *Other medicaments*

(a)   Preparations for external application:

   An antiseptic for use in wounds.
   A disinfectant.
   An insecticide.
   A liniment.
   A lotion for acute dermatitis.
   An ointment for haemorrhoids.
   A preparation for ringworm, such as compound of benzoic and salicylic acid.
   A preparation for chronic skin inflammations, e.g. compound zinc oxide paste.

----

[1] It is recommended that medicaments given by injection and included in this list, such as adrenalin, should whenever possible be supplied in single-dose containers.
   * Optional.

A preparation for burns.

An application of benzyl benzoate for scabies.

* A venereal-disease prophylactic package.

(b) Preparations for use in the eye:

An anaesthetic.

An antiseptic.

* Yellow mercury oxide eye-ointment.

(c) A preparation for toothache.

(d) Preparations for internal use:

Tablets of barbituric acid derivatives: (i) short-acting and hypnotic; (ii) long-acting and sedative.

Tablets of hyoscine hydrobromide (scopolamine hydrobromide) or equivalent sea-sickness remedy.

Tablets of sodium chloride (for heat cramp).

An injection of repository form of penicillin, e.g. procaine penicillin G fortified (procaine penicillin G with crystalline penicillin), or PAM (procaine penicillin G in oil with aluminium monostearate), or benzathine penicillin G.

* An antibiotic for oral use, e.g. oxytetracycline hydrochloride or penicillin V.

* An antihistamine preparation.
Medicine to control gastric acidity.
Laxatives.

(e) Others:

Olive oil (or equivalent).

A copy of the *International list of venereal-disease treatment centres at ports*, published by the World Health Organization. Personal booklets for venereal-disease treatment in the form appended to the above publication.

Of the above list, the tablets of barbituric acid derivatives and of codeine phosphate, the injection of morphine and the tinctures of opium and of belladonna should be kept under lock and key by the master of the vessel or other responsible officer, who should also be responsible for the procaine and penicillin.

C. *Surgical instruments, appliances and equipment*

Thermometer.

Hypodermic syringe and needles (suitable both for serums and for other injections).

Suture and ligatures (catgut, silkworm gut).

Suture needles (and possibly a needle holder).

Haemostatic forceps.

Splinter forceps.

Dissecting forceps.

Scalpel (stainless).

Surgical scissors.

Tourniquet.

Eye spud.

Eye cup,

Droppers.

Soft-rubber catheters of various sizes.

---

* Optional.

Splints (wooden or wire).
Bedpan.
Urine bottle.
Kidney dish.
Feeding cup.
Hot-water bottle.
Stretcher (a type suitable for transferring patients from one part of the ship to another, such as the Neil-Robertson stretcher or equivalent).
Bandage scissors.
Wooden applicators.
Bandages.
Gauze.
Cotton wool.
Adhesive tape.
Elastic adhesive bandages.
* Plaster of Paris bandages.

Medical Advice at Sea Recommendation, 1958 (No. 106)

The Conference recommends that each Member should apply the following provisions:

Members should ensure by a prearranged system that –

(a) medical advice by radio to ships at sea is available free of charge at any hour of the day or night;

(b) the medical advice available includes, where necessary and practicable, specialist advice;

(c) adequate use is made of the radio advice facilities available, inter alia, by instruction of seagoing personnel and by medical-guides which indicate clearly and concisely the type of information which will help the doctor in giving his advice, so that the person on board ship who seeks advice understands what sort of information is required by the advising doctor;

(d) an up-to-date and complete list of radio stations from which medical advice can be obtained is carried on each ship equipped with radio installations, and kept in the custody of the radio officer or, in the case of smaller vessels, of the person responsible for radio duties.

---

* Optional.

LABOUR INSPECTION

Labour Inspection (Seamen) Recommendation, 1926 (No. 28)

Whereas among the methods and principles of special and urgent importance for the physical, moral and intellectual welfare of the workers, the Constitution of the International Labour Organization makes it a duty of the International Labour Organization to devote special attention to the inspection of conditions of work in order to ensure the enforcement of the laws and regulations for the protection of the workers,

Whereas the International Labour Conference at its Fifth Session (October 1923) adopted a "Recommendation concerning the general principles for the organization of systems of inspection to secure the enforcement of the laws and regulations for the protection of the workers",

Whereas that Recommendation is based essentially on the experience gained in the inspection of industrial establishments and it would be particularly difficult to apply or even to adapt it to the work of seamen, the nature and conditions of which are essentially different from those of work in a factory,

Whereas the inspection of the conditions under which seamen work will increase in importance in proportion as legislation for the protection of seamen is developed in the different countries and as further Conventions concerning the working conditions of seamen are adopted by the Conference,

Whereas for the foregoing reasons it is desirable, in order to place the experience already gained at the disposal of the Members with a view to assisting them in the institution or reorganization of their systems of inspection of the conditions under which seamen work, to indicate the general principles which practice shows to be best calculated to ensure the enforcement of measures for the protection of seamen;

The General Conference therefore recommends that each Member of the Organization should take the following principles into consideration:

I. SCOPE OF INSPECTION

1. That the principal duty of the authority or authorities responsible in each country for the inspection of the conditions under which seamen work should be to secure the enforcement of all laws and regulations dealing with such conditions and the protection of seamen in the exercise of their profession;

2. That, in so far as it may be considered desirable and possible, by reason of the experience they gain in carrying out their principal duties, to entrust the inspecting authorities with other secondary duties of a social nature which may vary according to the conceptions, customs, or traditions prevailing in the different countries, such duties may be assigned to them in addition to their principal duties on condition that –

(a) they do not in any way interfere with the performance of the inspectors' principal duties;

(b) they do not in any way prejudice the authority and impartiality which are necessary to inspectors in their relations with shipowners and seamen.

II. ORGANIZATION OF INSPECTION

The Conference recommends:

3. That, wherever it is compatible with administrative practice and in order to secure the greatest possible uniformity in the enforcement of the laws and regulations relating to the conditions under which seamen work, the different services or bodies responsible for supervising the enforcement of such laws and regulations should be centralized under a single authority;

4. That, if existing administrative practice will not admit of such centralization of supervision, the different services or authorities whose functions are wholly or partly concerned with the protection of seamen should be enabled to benefit by one another's experience and to regulate their methods of work according to such common principles as may be considered the most effective;

5. That for this purpose close liaison and constant collaboration should be established between these different services or authorities, so far as is compatible with administrative practice and by the means considered the most suitable in each country (exchange of reports and information, periodical conferences, etc.); and

6. That the different services or authorities responsible for supervising the conditions under which seamen work should keep in touch with the authorities responsible for factory inspection, in matters of mutual concern.

III. REPORT OF THE INSPECTION AUTHORITIES

The Conference recommends:

7. That an annual general report on the supervision of the conditions under which seamen work should be published by the central authority or by the collaboration of the different authorities responsible for carrying out such supervision;

8. That this annual report should contain a list of the national laws and regulations affecting the conditions under which seamen work and their supervision,

together with any amendments thereto, which have come into operation during the year;

9.   That it should also contain statistical tables with the necessary comments on the organization and work of inspection and giving information, as far as may be possible and compatible with national administrative practice, on the following points:

(a)   the number of vessels in commission subject to the various forms of inspection, the vessels being classified according to type (mechanically propelled vessels and sailing vessels) and each category being subdivided according to the purpose for which these vessels are used;

(b)   the number of seamen actually engaged on board the vessels of each class;

(c)   the number of vessels visited by the inspectors with an indication of the strength of the crews;

(d)   the number and nature of breaches of the law or regulations ascertained by the inspectors and of the penalties imposed;

(e)   the number, nature, and causes of accidents occurring to seamen during their work;

(f)   the means adopted for the enforcement of the provisions of international labour Conventions which relate to the conditions under which seamen work, and the extent of the compliance with such provisions, either in the form of the annual report transmitted to the International Labour Office under Article 22 of the Constitution of the International Labour Organization or in some other appropriate form.

IV.   Rights, power and duties of inspectors

(a)   *Rights of inspection*

The Conference recommends:

10.   That the inspection authorities, on proof of their identity, should be empowered by national law:

(a)   to visit without previous notice any vessel flying the national flag by day or by night, in national or foreign territorial waters, and, in exceptional cases fixed by national law and by authorization of the maritime authority, at sea, provided, however, that the time and manner of such visits should in practice be fixed so as to avoid as far as possible any serious inconvenience to the working of the vessel;

(b)   to question without witnesses the crew and any other persons whose evidence may be considered desirable, to make any enquiries which may be judged necessary, and to require production of any of the ship's papers or documents which the laws or regulations require to be kept in so far as such papers or documents relate to the matters subject to inspection;

11.   That national law should provide that the inspectors should be bound by oath, or by any other method which conforms with the administrative practice or

customs in each country, not to disclose commercial secrets which may come to their knowledge in the course of their duties, under pain of criminal penalties or appropriate disciplinary measures.

(b) *Compulsory powers*

The Conference recommends:

12. That the inspection authorities should be empowered, in serious cases where the health or safety of the crew is endangered, to prohibit by proper authorization of the maritime authority a vessel from leaving port until the necessary measures have been taken on board to comply with the law, subject to appeal to higher administrative authority or to the court of competent jurisdiction, according to the law in the different countries;

13. That prohibiting a vessel from leaving port should be considered a measure of exceptional gravity, which should only be employed as a last resort when the other legal means at the disposal of the inspection authority to ensure respect for the law have been used without effect;

14. That the inspection authorities should be empowered in special cases to issue orders for securing observance of the laws and regulations governing the conditions under which seamen work, subject to appeal to higher administrative authority or to the court of competent jurisdiction, according to the law in each country;

15. That the central authority should be empowered in special cases to grant exemption from any specified requirement of any law or regulation governing the conditions under which seamen work, if such authority is satisfied that that requirement has been substantially complied with, or that compliance with the requirement is unnecessary in the circumstances of the case, and that the action taken, or provision made, as regards the subject matter of the requirement is as effective as, or more effective than, actual compliance with the requirement.

(c) *Right to call for an inspection*

The Conference recommends:

16. That national law should provide that the master of a vessel should be entitled to call for an inspection in all cases where he considers it necessary;

17. That national law should provide that the members of the crew of a vessel should also be entitled, subject to such conditions as may be prescribed, to call for an inspection on any matters relating to health, the safety of the vessel, or the rules affecting the conditions under which seamen work.

(d) *Cooperation of shipowners and seamen with the inspection authorities*

The Conference recommends:

18. That, so far as is compatible with administrative practice in each country, and by such methods as may be considered most appropriate, shipowners and

seamen should be called upon to cooperate in the supervision of the enforcement of the laws and regulations relating to the conditions under which seamen work;

In particular, the Conference draws the attention of the different countries to the following methods of cooperation:

(a)   it is essential that every facility should be afforded to seamen freely to bring to the notice of the inspection authorities either directly or through their duly authorized representatives any infringement of the law on board the vessel on which such seamen are employed, that the inspection authority should as far as possible promptly make an enquiry into the subject matter of any such complaint, that such complaints should be treated by the inspection authority as absolutely confidential;

(b)   with a view to ensuring complete cooperation by shipowners and seamen and their respective organizations with the inspection authorities, and in order to improve conditions affecting the health and safety of seamen, it is desirable that the inspection authorities should from time to time consult the representatives of shipowners' and seamen's organizations as to the best means of attaining these ends. It is also desirable that joint committees of shipowners and seamen should be set up, and that they should be enabled to cooperate with the different services responsible for supervising the enforcement of the laws and regulations governing the conditions under which seamen work.

(e)   *Safeguards*

The Conference recommends:

19.   That only such persons should be appointed inspectors as command the full confidence both of the shipowners and of the seamen and that such persons should therefore be required to possess:

(a)   the qualities necessary to ensure absolute impartiality in the performance of their duties;

(b)   the technical qualifications necessary for the performance of their duties;

It is desirable that the inspection service should include men who have served at sea whose appointment whether in a permanent or temporary capacity should be at the discretion of the administrative authority;

20.   That, when necessary, inspectors should be assisted in their duties by competent experts who command the full confidence of the shipowners and seamen;

21.   That inspectors should be public servants, whose status renders them independent of changes of Government;

22.   That they should be prohibited from having any financial interest whatsoever in the undertakings subject to their inspection.

(f)   *Other duties*

The Conference recommends:

23.   That as, by reason of the nature of their duties, inspectors have special opportunities of observing the practical results of the operation of the laws and

regulations governing the conditions under which seamen work, they should be called upon, so far as it is compatible with the administrative methods in each country, to assist in improving legislation for the protection of seamen and to give the most effectual help possible in promoting the prevention of accidents;

24. That, so far as is compatible with administrative practice in each country, they should be called upon to take part in enquiries into shipwrecks and accidents on board ship, and that they should be empowered, where necessary, to submit reports on the results of such enquiries;

25. That, so far as is compatible with the administrative methods in each country, they should be called upon to collaborate in supplying information preparatory to the drafting of laws and regulations for the protection of seamen.

SOCIAL SECURITY

Unemployment Indemnity (Shipwreck) Convention, 1920 (No. 8)

Date of entry into force: 16 March 1923

Article 1

1.   For the purpose of this Convention, the term "seamen" includes all persons employed on any vessel engaged in maritime navigation.

2.   For the purpose of this Convention, the term "vessel" includes all ships and boats, of any nature whatsoever, engaged in maritime navigation, whether publicly or privately owned; it excludes ships of war.

Article 2

1.   In every case of loss or foundering of any vessel, the owner or person with whom the seaman has contracted for service on board the vessel shall pay to each seaman employed thereon an indemnity against unemployment resulting from such loss or foundering.

2.   This indemnity shall be paid for the days during which the seaman remains in fact unemployed at the same rate as the wages payable under the contract, but the total indemnity payable under this Convention to any one seaman may be limited to two months' wages.

Article 3

Seamen shall have the same remedies for recovering such indemnities as they have for recovering arrears of wages earned during the service.

* * *

Articles 6 and 7: Entry into force immediately following registration of two ratifications. Thereafter, entry into force for other Members on the date on which their ratification is registered.

* * *

Article 9: Denunciation: this Convention became open to denunciation five years after it first came into force.

Unemployment Insurance (Seamen) Recommendation 1920 (No. 10)

The General Conference, with a view to securing the application to seamen of Part III of the Recommendation concerning unemployment adopted at Washington on 28 November 1919, recommends that each Member of the International Labour Organization should establish for seamen an effective system of insurance against unemployment arising out of shipwreck or any other cause, either by means of Government insurance or by means of Government subventions to industrial organizations whose rules provide for the payment of benefits to their unemployed members.

Shipowners' Liability (Sick and Injured Seamen) Convention, 1936 (No. 55)

Date of entry into force: 29 October 1939

Article 1

1. This Convention applies to all persons employed on board any vessel, other than a ship of war, registered in a territory for which this Convention is in force and ordinarily engaged in maritime navigation.

2. Provided that any Member of the International Labour Organization may in its national laws or regulations make such exceptions as it deems necessary in respect of:

(a) persons employed on board,

    (i) vessels of public authorities when such vessels are not engaged in trade;

    (ii) coastwise fishing boats;

    (iii) boats of less than twenty-five tons gross tonnage;

    (iv) wooden ships of primitive build such as dhows and junks;

(b) persons employed on board by an employer other than the shipowner;

(c) persons employed solely in ports in repairing, cleaning, loading or unloading vessels;

(d) members of the shipowner's family;

(e) pilots.

Article 2

1. The shipowner shall be liable in respect of –

(a) sickness and injury occurring between the date specified in the articles of agreement for reporting for duty and the termination of the engagement;

(b) death resulting from such sickness or injury.

2. Provided that national laws or regulations may make exceptions in respect of –

(a) injury incurred otherwise than in the service of the ship;

(b) injury or sickness due to the wilful act, default or misbehaviour of the sick, injured or deceased person;

(c)   sickness or infirmity intentionally concealed when the engagement is entered into.

3.   National laws or regulations may provide that the shipowner shall not be liable in respect of sickness, or death directly attributable to sickness, if at the time of the engagement the person employed refused to be medically examined.

Article 3

For the purpose of this Convention, medical care and maintenance at the expense of the shipowner comprises –

(a)   medical treatment and the supply of proper and sufficient medicines and therapeutical appliances; and

(b)   board and lodging.

Article 4

1.   The shipowner shall be liable to defray the expense of medical care and maintenance until the sick or injured person has been cured, or until the sickness or incapacity has been declared of a permanent character.

2.   Provided that national laws or regulations may limit the liability of the shipowner to defray the expense of medical care and maintenance to a period which shall not be less than sixteen weeks from the day of the injury or the commencement of the sickness.

3.   Provided also that, if there is in force in the territory in which the vessel is registered a scheme applying to seamen of compulsory sickness insurance, compulsory accident insurance or workmen's compensation for accidents, national laws or regulations may provide –

(a)   that a shipowner shall cease to be liable in respect of a sick or injured person from the time at which that person becomes entitled to medical benefits under the insurance or compensation scheme;

(b)   that the shipowner shall cease to be liable from the time prescribed by law for the grant of medical benefits under the insurance or compensation scheme to the beneficiaries of such schemes, even when the sick or injured person is not covered by the scheme in question, unless he is excluded from the scheme by reason of any restriction which affects particularly foreign workers or workers not resident in the territory in which the vessel is registered.

Article 5

1.   Where the sickness or injury results in incapacity for work the shipowner shall be liable –

(a)   to pay full wages as long as the sick or injured person remains on board;

(b)   if the sick or injured person has dependants, to pay wages in whole or in part as prescribed by national laws or regulations from the time when he is landed until he has been cured or the sickness or incapacity has been declared of a permanent character.

2.   Provided that national laws or regulations may limit the liability of the shipowner to pay wages in whole or in part in respect of a person no longer on board to a period which shall not be less than sixteen weeks from the day of the injury or the commencement of the sickness.

3.   Provided also that, if there is in force in the territory in which the vessel is registered a scheme applying to seamen of compulsory sickness insurance, compulsory accident insurance or workmen's compensation for accidents, national laws or regulations may provide:

(a)   that a shipowner shall cease to be liable in respect of a sick or injured person from the time at which that person becomes entitled to cash benefits under the insurance or compensation scheme;

(b)   that the shipowner shall cease to be liable from the time prescribed by law for the grant of cash benefits under the insurance or compensation scheme to the beneficiaries of such schemes, even when the sick or injured person is not covered by the scheme in question, unless he is excluded from the scheme by reason of any restriction which affects particularly foreign workers or workers not resident in the territory in which the vessel is registered.

Article 6

1.   The shipowner shall be liable to defray the expense of repatriating every sick or injured person who is landed during the voyage in consequence of sickness or injury.

2.   The port to which the sick or injured person is to be returned shall be –

(a)   the port at which he was engaged; or

(b)   the port at which the voyage commenced; or

(c)   a port in his own country or the country to which he belongs; or

(d)   another port agreed upon by him and the master or shipowner, with the approval of the competent authority.

3.   The expense of repatriation shall include all charges for the transportation, accommodation and food of the sick or injured person during the journey and his maintenance up to the time fixed for his departure.

4.   If the sick or injured person is capable of work, the shipowner may discharge his liability to repatriate him by providing him with suitable employment on board a vessel proceeding to one of the destinations mentioned in paragraph 2 of this Article.

Article 7

1.   The shipowner shall be liable to defray burial expenses in case of death occurring on board, or in case of death occurring on shore if at the time of his death the deceased person was entitled to medical care and maintenance at the shipowner's expense.

2.   National laws or regulations may provide that burial expenses paid by the shipowner shall be reimbursed by an insurance institution in cases in which

funeral benefit is payable in respect of the deceased person under laws or regulations relating to social insurance or workmen's compensation.

Article 8

National laws or regulations shall require the shipowner or his representative to take measures for safeguarding property left on board by sick, injured or deceased persons to whom this Convention applies.

Article 9

National laws or regulations shall make provision for securing the rapid and inexpensive settlement of disputes concerning the liability of the shipowner under this Convention.

Article 10

The shipowner may be exempted from liability under Articles 4, 6 and 7 of this Convention in so far as such liability is assumed by the public authorities.

Article 11

This Convention and national laws or regulations relating to benefits under this Convention shall be so interpreted and enforced as to ensure equality of treatment to all seamen irrespective of nationality, domicile or race.

Article 12

Nothing in this Convention shall affect any law, award, custom or agreement between shipowners and seamen which ensures more favourable conditions than those provided by this Convention.

Sickness Insurance (Sea) Convention, 1936 (No. 56)

Date of entry into force: 9 December 1949

Article 1

1.   Every person employed as master or member of the crew or otherwise in the service of the ship, on board any vessel, other than a ship of war, registered in a territory for which this Convention is in force and engaged in maritime navigation or sea-fishing, shall be insured under a compulsory sickness insurance scheme.

2.   Provided that any Member of the International Labour Organization may in its national laws or regulations make such exceptions as it deems necessary in respect of –

(a) persons employed on board vessels of public authorities when such vessels are not engaged in trade;

(b) persons whose wages or income exceed a prescribed amount;

(c) persons who are not paid a money wage;

(d) persons not resident in the territory of the Member;

(e) persons below or above prescribed age-limits;

(f) members of the employer's family;

(g) pilots.

Article 2

1.   An insured person who is rendered incapable of work and deprived of his wages by reason of sickness shall be entitled to a cash benefit for at least the first twenty-six weeks or one hundred and eighty days of incapacity from and including the first day for which benefit is payable.

2.   The right to benefit may be made conditional upon the completion of a qualifying period and of a waiting period of a few days to be counted from the beginning of the incapacity.

3.   The cash benefit granted to the insured person shall never be fixed at a rate lower than that fixed by the general scheme of compulsory sickness insurance, where such a scheme exists but does not apply to seamen.

4.   Cash benefit may be withheld –

(a) while the insured person is on board or abroad;

(b) while the insured person is maintained by the insurance institution or from public funds. Provided that in such case it shall only partially be withheld when the insured person has family responsibilities;

(c) while in respect of the same illness the insured person receives compensation from another source to which he is entitled by law, so however that in such case benefit shall only be wholly or partially withheld if and so far as such compensation is equal to or less than the amount of the benefit payable under the sickness insurance scheme.

5.   Cash benefit may be reduced or refused in the case of sickness caused by the insured person's wilful misconduct.

Article 3

1.   The insured person shall be entitled free of charge, as from the commencement of his illness and at least until the period prescribed for the grant of sickness benefit expires, to medical treatment by a fully qualified medical practitioner and to the supply of proper and sufficient medicines and appliances.

2.   Provided that the insured person may be required to pay such part of the cost of medical benefit as may be prescribed by national laws or regulations.

3.   Medical benefit may be withheld while the insured person is on board or abroad.

4.   Whenever the circumstances so require, the insurance institution may provide for the treatment of the sick person in hospital and in such case shall grant him full maintenance, together with the necessary medical attention and care.

Article 4

1.   When the insured person is abroad and by reason of sickness has lost his right to wages, whether previously payable in whole or in part, the cash benefit to which he would have been entitled had he not been abroad shall be paid in whole or in part to his family until his return to the territory of the Member.

2.   National laws or regulations may prescribe or authorize the provision of the following benefits:

(a) when the insured person has family responsibilities, a cash benefit additional to that provided for in Article 2;

(b) in case of the sickness of members of the insured person's family living in his home and dependent on him, aid in kind or in cash.

Article 5

1.   National laws or regulations shall prescribe the conditions under which an insured woman, while in the territory of the Member, shall be entitled to maternity benefit.

2.   National laws or regulations may prescribe the conditions under which the wife of an insured man, while in the territory of the Member, shall be entitled to maternity benefit.

Article 6

1.   On the death of the insured person, a cash benefit of an amount prescribed by national laws or regulations shall be paid to the members of the family of the deceased or be applied for defraying the funeral expenses.

2.   Where there is in force a pension scheme for the survivors of deceased seamen, the grant of the cash benefit provided for in the preceding paragraph shall not be compulsory.

Article 7

The right to insurance benefit shall continue even in respect of sickness occurring during a definite period after the termination of the last engagement, which period shall be fixed by national laws or regulations in such a way as to cover the normal interval between successive engagements.

Article 8

1.   The insured persons and their employers shall share in providing the financial resources of the sickness insurance scheme.

2.   National laws or regulations may provide for a financial contribution by the public authorities.

Article 9

1.   Sickness insurance shall be administered by self-governing institutions, which shall be under the administrative and financial supervision of the public authorities and shall not be carried on with a view to profit.

2.   Insured persons, and in the case of insurance institutions set up specially for seamen under laws or regulations the employers also, shall participate in the management of the institutions under such conditions as may be prescribed by national laws or regulations, which may also provide for the participation of other persons concerned.

3.   Provided that the administration of sickness insurance may be undertaken directly by the State where and so long as its administration by self-governing institutions is rendered difficult or impossible by reason of national conditions.

Article 10

1.   The insured person shall have a right of appeal in case of dispute concerning his right to benefit.

2.   The procedure for dealing with disputes shall be rendered rapid and inexpensive for the insured person by means of special courts or any other method deemed appropriate under national laws or regulations.

Article 11

Nothing in this Convention shall affect any law, award, custom or agreement between shipowners and seamen which ensures more favourable conditions than those provided by this Convention.

* * *

Articles 14 and 18: Entry into force and revision: the Convention is closed to further ratification since the entry into force of Convention No 165, which revises it.

Social Security (Seafarers) Convention (Revised), 1987 (No. 165)

Date of entry into force: 2 July 1992

PART I.   GENERAL PROVISIONS

Article 1

In this Convention –

(a)   the term "Member" means any Member of the International Labour Organization that is bound by the Convention;

(b)   the term "legislation" includes any social security rules as well as laws and regulations;

(c)   the term "seafarers" means persons employed in any capacity on board a seagoing ship which is engaged in the transport of cargo or passengers for the purpose of trade, is utilized for any other commercial purpose or is a seagoing tug, with the exception of persons employed on –

   (i)   small vessels including those primarily propelled by sail, whether or not they are fitted with auxiliary engines;

   (ii)   vessels such as oil rigs and drilling platforms when not engaged in navigation;

   the decision as to which vessels and installations are covered by clauses (i) and (ii) being taken by the competent authority of each Member in consultation with the most representative organizations of shipowners and seafarers;

(d)   the term "dependant" has the meaning assigned to it by national legislation;

(e)   the term "survivors" means persons defined or recognized as such by the legislation under which the benefits are awarded; where persons are defined or recognized as survivors under the relevant legislation only on the condition that they were living with the deceased, this condition shall be deemed to be satisfied in respect of persons who obtained their main support from the deceased;

(f)   the term "competent Member" means the Member under whose legislation the person concerned can claim benefit;

(g)   the term "residence" and "resident" refer to ordinary residence;

(h)   the term "temporarily resident" refers to a temporary stay;

(i)   the term "repatriation" means transportation to a place to which seafarers are entitled to be returned under laws and regulations or collective agreements applicable to them;

(j)   the term "non-contributory" applies to benefits the award of which does not depend on direct financial participation by the persons protected or by their employer, or on a qualifying period of occupational activity;

(k)   the term "refugee" has the meaning assigned to it in Article 1 of the Convention relating to the Status of Refugees of 28 July 1951 and in paragraph 2 of Article 1 of the Protocol relating to the Status of Refugees of 31 January 1967;

(l)   the term "stateless person" has the meaning assigned to it in Article 1 of the Convention relating to the Status of Stateless Persons of 28 September 1954.

Article 2

1.   The Convention applies to all seafarers and, where applicable, their dependants and their survivors.

2.   To the extent it deems practicable, after consultation with the representative organizations of fishing vessel owners and fishermen, the competent authority shall apply the provisions of this Convention to commercial maritime fishing.

Article 3

Members are bound to comply with the provisions of Article 9 or Article 11 in respect of at least three of the following branches of social security:

(a)   medical care;

(b)   sickness benefit;

(c)   unemployment benefit;

(d)   old-age benefit;

(e)   employment injury benefit;

(f)   family benefit;

(g)   maternity benefit;

(h)   invalidity benefit;

(i)   survivors' benefit; including at least one of the branches specified in subparagraphs (c), (d), (e), (h) and (i).

Article 4

Each Member shall specify at the time of its ratification in respect of which of the branches mentioned in Article 3 it accepts the obligations of Article 9 or Article 11, and shall indicate separately in respect of each of the branches specified whether it undertakes to apply the minimum standards of Article 9 or the superior standards of Article 11 to that branch.

Article 5

Each Member may subsequently notify the Director-General of the International Labour Office that it accepts, with effect from the date of the notification, the obligations of this Convention in respect of one or more of the branches mentioned in Article 3 not already specified at the time of its ratification, indicating separately in respect of each of these branches whether it undertakes to apply to that branch the minimum standards of Article 9 or the superior standards of Article 11.

Article 6

A Member may by a notification to the Director-General of the International Labour Office, which shall take effect as from the date of the notification, subsequently replace the application of the provisions of Article 9 by that of the provisions of Article 11 in respect of any branch accepted.

PART II. PROTECTION PROVIDED
GENERAL STANDARDS

Article 7

The legislation of each Member shall provide for seafarers to whom the legislation of that Member is applicable social security protection not less favourable than that enjoyed by shoreworkers in respect of each of the branches of social security mentioned in Article 3 for which it has legislation in force.

Article 8

Arrangements for the maintenance of rights in course of acquisition by a person who, having ceased to be subject to a Member's scheme of compulsory social security for seafarers, becomes subject to an equivalent scheme of that Member for shoreworkers, or vice versa, shall be made between the schemes concerned.

MINIMUM STANDARDS

Article 9

When a Member has undertaken to apply the provisions of this Article to any branch of social security, seafarers and, where applicable, their dependants and survivors who are protected by the legislation of that Member shall be entitled to social security benefits not less favourable in respect of contingencies covered, conditions of award, level and duration than those specified in the following provisions of the Social Security (Minimum Standards) Convention, 1952, for the branch in question:

(a) for *medical care* in Articles 8, 10 (paragraphs 1, 2 and 3), 11 and 12 (paragraph 1);

(b) for *sickness benefit* in Articles 14, 16 (in conjunction with Article 65 or 66 or 67), 17 and 18 (paragraph 1);

(c) for *unemployment benefit* in Articles 20, 22 (in conjunction with Article 65 or 66 or 67), 23 and 24;

(d) for *old-age benefit* in Articles 26, 28 (in conjunction with Article 65 or 66 or 67), 29 and 30;

(e) for *employment injury benefit* in Articles 32, 34 (paragraphs 1, 2 and 4), 35, 36 (in conjunction with Article 65 or 66) and 38;

(f) for *family benefit* in Articles 40, 42, 43, 44 (in conjunction with Article 66, where applicable) and 45;

(g) for *maternity benefit* in Articles 47, 49 (paragraphs 1, 2 and 3), 50 (in conjunction with Article 65 or 66), 51 and 52;

(h) for *invalidity benefit* in Articles 54, 56 (in conjunction with Article 65 or 66 or 67), 57 and 58;

(i) for *survivors' benefit* in Articles 60, 62 (in conjunction with Article 65 or 66 or 67), 63 and 64.

Article 10

For the purpose of compliance with the provisions of subparagraphs (a), (b), (c), (d), (g) (as regards medical care), (h) or (i) of Article 9, a Member may take account of protection effected by means of insurance which is not made compulsory for seafarers by its legislation when this insurance –

(a) is supervised by the public authorities or administered, in accordance with prescribed standards, by joint operation of shipowners and seafarers;

(b) covers a substantial proportion of the seafarers whose earnings do not exceed those of a skilled employee; and

(c) complies, in conjunction with other forms of protection where appropriate, with the relevant provisions of the Social Security (Minimum Standards) Convention, 1952.

SUPERIOR STANDARDS

Article 11

When a Member has undertaken to apply the provisions of this Article to any branch of social security, seafarers and, where applicable, their dependants and survivors who are protected by the legislation of that Member shall be entitled to social security benefits not less favourable in respect of contingencies covered, conditions of award, level and duration than those specified –

(a) for *medical care* in Articles 7 (a), 8, 9, 13, 15, 16 and 17 of the Medical Care and Sickness Benefits Convention, 1969;

(b) for *sickness benefit* in Articles 7 (b), 18, 21 (in conjunction with Article 22 or 23 or 24), 25 and 26 (paragraphs 1 and 3) of the Medical Care and Sickness Benefits Convention, 1969;

(c) for *old-age benefit* in Articles 15, 17 (in conjunction with Article 26 or 27 or 28), 18, 19 and 29 (paragraph 1) of the Invalidity, Old-Age and Survivors' Benefits Convention, 1967;

(d) for *employment injury benefit* in Articles 6, 9 (paragraphs 2 and 3 (introductory sentence)), 10, 13 (in conjunction with Article 19 or 20), 14 (in conjunction with Article 19 or 20), 15 (paragraph 1), 16, 17, 18 (paragraphs 1 and 2) (in conjunction with Article 19 or 20) and 21 (paragraph 1) of the Employment Injury Benefits Convention, 1964;

(e) for *maternity benefit* in Articles 3 and 4 of the Maternity Protection Convention (Revised), 1952;

(f) for *invalidity benefit* in Articles 8, 10 (in conjunction with Article 26 or 27 or 28), 11, 12, 13 and 29 (paragraph 1) of the Invalidity, Old-Age and Survivors' Benefits Convention, 1967;

(g) for *survivors' benefit* in Articles 21, 23 (in conjunction with Article 26 or 27 or 28), 24, 25 and 29 (paragraph 1) of the Invalidity, Old-Age and Survivors' Benefits Convention, 1967;

(h) for *unemployment benefit* and *family benefit* in any future Convention laying down standards superior to those specified in subparagraphs (c) and (f) of Article 9 which the General Conference of the International Labour Organization has, after its coming into force, recognized as applicable for the purpose of this clause by means of a Protocol adopted in the framework of a special maritime question included in its agenda.

Article 12

For the purpose of compliance with the provisions of subparagraphs (a), (b), (c), (e) (as regards medical care), (f), (g) or (h) (unemployment benefit) of Article 11, a Member may take account of protection effected by means of insurance which is not made compulsory for seafarers by its legislation when this insurance –

(a) is supervised by the public authorities or administered, in accordance with prescribed standards, by joint operation of shipowners and seafarers;

(b) covers a substantial proportion of the seafarers whose earnings do not exceed those of a skilled employee; and

(c) complies, in conjunction with other forms of protection, where appropriate, with the provisions of the Conventions referred to in the above-mentioned clauses of Article 11.

PART III. SHIPOWNER'S LIABILITY

Article 13

The shipowner shall be required to provide to seafarers whose condition requires medical care while they are on board or who are left behind by reason of their condition in the territory of a State other than the competent Member –

(a) proper and sufficient medical care until their recovery or until their repatriation, whichever first occurs;

(b) board and lodging until they are able to obtain suitable employment or are repatriated, whichever first occurs; and

(c) repatriation.

Article 14

Seafarers who by reason of their condition are left behind in the territory of a State other than the competent Member shall continue to be entitled to their full wages (exclusive of bonuses) from the time when they are left behind until they receive an offer of suitable employment, or until they are repatriated, or until the expiry of a period of a length (which shall not be less than 12 weeks) prescribed by the national laws or regulations of that Member or by collective agreement, whichever event first occurs. The shipowner shall cease to be liable for the payment of wages from the time such seafarers are entitled to cash benefits under the legislation of the competent Member.

Article 15

Seafarers who by reason of their condition are repatriated or are landed in the territory of the competent Member shall continue to be entitled to their full wages (exclusive of bonuses) from the time when they are repatriated or landed until their recovery, or until the expiry of a period of a length (which shall not be less than 12 weeks) prescribed by the national laws or regulations of that Member or by collective agreement, whichever event first occurs. Any period during which wages were paid by virtue of Article 14 shall be deducted from such period. The shipowner shall cease to be liable for the payment of wages from the time such seafarers are entitled to cash benefits under the legislation of the competent Member.

PART IV. PROTECTION OF FOREIGN OR MIGRANT SEAFARERS

Article 16

The following rules shall apply to seafarers who are or have been subject to the legislation of one or more Members, as well as, where applicable, to their dependants and their survivors, in respect of any branch of social security specified in Article 3 for which any such Member has legislation applicable to seafarers in force.

Article 17

With a view to avoiding conflicts of laws and the undesirable consequences that might ensue for those concerned either through lack of protection or as a result of undue plurality of contributions or other liabilities or of benefits, the legislation applicable in respect of seafarers shall be determined by the Members concerned in accordance with the following rules:

(a) seafarers shall be subject to the legislation of one Member only;

(b) in principle this legislation shall be:

  – the legislation of the Member whose flag the ship is flying, or

  – the legislation of the Member in whose territory the seafarer is resident;

(c) notwithstanding the rules set forth in the preceding subparagraphs, Members concerned may determine, by mutual agreement, other rules concerning the legislation applicable to seafarers, in the interest of the persons concerned.

Article 18

Seafarers who are subject to the legislation of a Member and are nationals of another Member, or are refugees or stateless persons resident in the territory of a Member, shall enjoy under that legislation equality of treatment with the nationals of the first Member, both as regards coverage and as regards the right to benefits. They shall enjoy equality of treatment without any condition of residence on the territory of the first Member if its nationals are protected without any such condition. This requirement shall also apply, where appropriate, as regards the right to benefit of seafarers' dependants and survivors irrespective of their nationality.

Article 19

Notwithstanding the provisions of Article 18, the award of non-contributory benefits may be made conditional on the beneficiary having resided in the territory of the competent Member or, in the case of survivors' benefit, on the deceased having resided there for a period which may not be set at more than –

(a) six months immediately preceding the lodging of the claim, for unemployment benefit and maternity benefit;

(b) five consecutive years immediately preceding the lodging of the claim, for invalidity benefit, or immediately preceding the death, for survivors' benefit;

(c) ten years between the age of 18 and the pensionable age, of which it may be required that five years shall immediately precede the lodging of the claim, for old-age benefit.

Article 20

The laws and regulations of each Member relating to shipowners' liability provided for in Articles 13 to 15 shall ensure equality of treatment to seafarers irrespective of their place of residence.

Article 21

Each Member shall endeavour to participate with every other Member concerned in schemes for the maintenance of rights in course of acquisition, as regards each branch of social security specified in Article 3, for which each of these Members has legislation in force, for the benefit of persons who have been subject successively or alternately, in the capacity of seafarers, to the legislation of the said Members.

Article 22

The schemes for the maintenance of rights in course of acquisition referred to in Article 21 shall provide for the adding together, to the extent necessary, of periods of insurance, employment or residence, as the case may be, completed under the legislation of the Members concerned for the purposes of acquisition, maintenance or recovery of rights and, as the case may be, calculation of benefits.

Article 23

The schemes for the maintenance of rights in course of acquisition referred to in Article 21 shall determine the formula for awarding invalidity, old-age and survivors' benefits, as well as the apportionment, where appropriate, of the costs involved.

Article 24

Each Member shall guarantee the provision of invalidity, old-age and survivors' cash benefits, pensions in respect of employment injuries and death grants, to which a right is acquired under its legislation, to beneficiaries who are nationals of a Member or refugees or stateless persons, irrespective of their place of residence, subject to measures for this purpose being taken, where necessary, by agreement between the Members or with the States concerned.

Article 25

Notwithstanding the provisions of Article 24, in the case of non-contributory benefits the Members concerned shall determine by mutual agreement the conditions under which the provision of these benefits shall be guaranteed to beneficiaries resident outside the territory of the competent Member.

Article 26

A Member having accepted the obligations of the Equality of Treatment (Social Security) Convention, 1962, for one or more of the branches of social security referred to in Article 24, but not those of the Maintenance of Social Security Rights Convention, 1982, may, in respect of each branch for which it has accepted the obligations of the first-mentioned Convention, derogate from the provisions of Article 24 and apply in its place the provisions of Article 5 of that Convention.

Article 27

Members concerned shall endeavour to participate in schemes for the maintenance of rights acquired under their legislation as regards each of the following branches of social security for which each of these Members has legislation applicable to seafarers in force: medical care, sickness benefit, unemployment benefit, employment injury benefits other than pensions and death grants, family benefit and maternity benefit. These schemes shall guarantee such benefits to persons resident or temporarily resident in the territory of one of these Members other than the competent Member, under conditions and within limits to be determined by mutual agreement between the Members concerned.

Article 28

The provisions of this Part do not apply to social and medical assistance.

Article 29

Members may derogate from the provisions of Articles 16 to 25 and Article 27 by making special arrangements in the framework of bilateral or multilateral instruments concluded amongst two or more of them, on condition that these do not affect the rights and obligations of other Members and provide for the protection of foreign or migrant seafarers in matters of social security under provisions which, in the aggregate, are at least as favourable as those required under these Articles.

PART V. LEGAL AND ADMINISTRATIVE SAFEGUARDS

Article 30

Every person concerned shall have the right of appeal in case of refusal of the benefit or complaint as to its nature, level, amount or quality.

Article 31

Where a government department responsible to a legislature is entrusted with the administration of medical care, every person concerned shall have a right, in addition to the right of appeal provided for in Article 30, to have a complaint concerning the refusal of medical care or the quality of the care received investigated by the appropriate authority.

Article 32

Each Member shall make provision for securing the rapid and inexpensive settlement of disputes concerning the shipowner's liability provided for in Articles 13 to 15.

Article 33

Members shall accept general responsibility for the due provision of the benefits provided in compliance with this Convention and shall take all measures required for this purpose.

Article 34

Members shall accept general responsibility for the proper administration of the institutions and services concerned in the application of this Convention.

Article 35

Where the administration is not entrusted to an institution regulated by the public authorities or to a government department responsible to a legislature –

(a) representatives of the seafarers protected shall participate in the management under conditions prescribed by national legislation;

(b) national legislation shall also, where appropriate, provide for the participation of representatives of the shipowners;

(c) national legislation may also provide for the participation of representatives of the public authorities.

PART VI. FINAL PROVISIONS

Article 36

This Convention revises the Sickness Insurance (Sea) Convention, 1936, and the Social Security (Seafarers) Convention, 1946.

Seafarers' Pensions Convention, 1946 (No. 71)

Date of entry into force: 10 October 1962

Article 1

In this Convention the term "seafarer" includes every person employed on board or in the service of any seagoing vessel other than a ship of war, which is registered in a territory for which the Convention is in force.

Article 2

1. Each Member of the International Labour Organization for which this Convention is in force shall, in accordance with national laws or regulations, establish or secure the establishment of a scheme for the payment of pensions to seafarers on retirement from sea service.

2. The scheme may embody such exceptions as the Member deems necessary in respect of:

(a) persons employed on board or in the service of:
   (i) vessels of public authorities when such vessels are not engaged in trade;
   (ii) vessels which are not engaged in the transport of cargo or passengers for the purpose of trade;
   (iii) fishing vessels;
   (iv) vessels engaged in hunting seals;
   (v) vessels of less than 200 gross register tons;
   (vi) wooden ships of primitive build such as dhows and junks;
   (vii) in so far as ships registered in India are concerned and for a period not exceeding five years from the date of the registration of the ratification of the Convention by India, home-trade vessels of a gross register tonnage not exceeding 300 tons;

(b) members of the shipowner's family;

(c) pilots not members of the crew;

(d) persons employed on board or in the service of the ship by an employer other than the shipowner, except radio officers or operators and catering staff;

(e) persons employed in port who are not ordinarily employed at sea;

(f) salaried employees in the service of a national public authority who are entitled to benefits at least equivalent on the whole to those provided for in this Convention;

(g) persons not remunerated for their services or remunerated only by a nominal salary or wage, or remunerated exclusively by a share of profits;

(h) persons working exclusively on their own account;

(i) persons employed on board or in the service of whale-catching, floating factory or transport vessels or otherwise for the purpose of whaling or similar operations under conditions regulated by the provisions of a special collective whaling or similar agreement determining the rates of pay, hours of work and other conditions of service concluded by an organization of seafarers concerned;

(j) persons not resident in the territory of the Member;

(k) persons not nationals of the Member.

Article 3

1. The scheme shall comply with one of the following conditions:

(a) the pensions provided by the scheme:

(i) shall be payable to seafarers having completed a prescribed period of sea service on attaining the age of fifty-five or sixty years as may be prescribed by the scheme; and

(ii) shall, together with any other social security pension payable simultaneously to the pensioner, be at a rate not less than the total obtained by computing for each year of his sea service 1.5 per cent of the remuneration on the basis of which contributions were paid in respect of him for that year if the scheme provides pensions on attaining the age of fifty-five years on 2 per cent of such remuneration if the scheme provides pensions at the age of sixty years; or

(b) the scheme shall provide pensions the financing of which, together with the financing of any other social security pension payable simultaneously to the pensioner and any social security benefits payable to the dependants (as defined by national laws or regulations) of deceased pensioners, requires a premium income from all sources which is not less than 10 per cent of the total remuneration on the basis of which contributions are paid to the scheme.

2. Seafarers collectively shall not contribute more than half the cost of the pensions payable under the scheme.

Article 4

1. The scheme shall make appropriate provision for the maintenance of rights in course of acquisition by persons ceasing to be subject thereto or for the payment to such persons of a benefit representing a return for the contributions credited to their account.

2. The scheme shall grant a right of appeal in any dispute arising thereunder.

3. The scheme may provide for the forfeiture or suspension of the right to a pension in whole or in part if the person concerned has acted fraudulently.

4. The shipowners and the seafarers who contribute to the cost of the pensions payable under the scheme shall be entitled to participate through representatives in the management of the scheme.

* * *

Article 6

1. This Convention shall be binding only upon those Members of the International Labour Organization whose ratifications have been registered with the Director-General.

2. It shall come into force six months after the date on which there have been registered ratifications by five of the following countries: United States of America, Argentine Republic, Australia, Belgium, Brazil, Canada, Chile, China, Denmark, Finland, France, United Kingdom of Great Britain and Northern Ireland, Greece, India, Ireland, Italy, Netherlands, Norway, Poland, Portugal, Sweden, Turkey and Yugoslavia, including at least three countries each of which has at least one million gross register tons of shipping. This provision is included for the purpose of facilitating and encouraging early ratification of the Convention by Member States.

3. Thereafter, this Convention shall come into force for any Member six months after the date on which its ratification has been registered.

INTERNATIONAL LABOUR STANDARDS APPLYING TO ALL WORKERS INCLUDING SEAFARERS

INTERNATIONAL LABOUR STANDARDS APPLYING TO ALL WORKERS INCLUDING SEAFARERS

Freedom of Association and Protection of the Right to Organize Convention, 1948 (No. 87)

Date of entry into force: 4 July 1950

PART I. FREEDOM OF ASSOCIATION

Article 1

Each Member of the International Labour Organization for which this Convention is in force undertakes to give effect to the following provisions.

Article 2

Workers and employers, without distinction whatsoever, shall have the right to establish and, subject only to the rules of the organization concerned, to join organizations of their own choosing without previous authorization.

Article 3

1. Workers' and employers' organizations shall have the right to draw up their constitutions and rules, to elect their representatives in full freedom, to organize their administration and activities and to formulate their programmes.

2. The public authorities shall refrain from any interference which would restrict this right or impede the lawful exercise thereof.

Article 4

Workers' and employers' organizations shall not be liable to be dissolved or suspended by administrative authority.

Article 5

Workers' and employers' organizations shall have the right to establish and join federations and confederations and any such organization, federation or confederation shall have the right to affiliate with international organizations of workers and employers.

Article 6

The provisions of Articles 2, 3 and 4 hereof apply to federations and confederations of workers' and employers' organizations.

Article 7

The acquisition of legal personality by workers' and employers' organizations, federations and confederations shall not be made subject to conditions of such a character as to restrict the application of the provisions of Articles 2, 3 and 4 hereof.

Article 8

1.　In exercising the rights provided for in this Convention workers and employers and their respective organizations, like other persons or organized collectivities, shall respect the law of the land.

2.　The law of the land shall not be such as to impair, nor shall it be so applied as to impair, the guarantees provided for in this Convention.

Article 9

1.　The extent to which the guarantees provided for in this Convention shall apply to the armed forces and the police shall be determined by national laws or regulations.

2.　In accordance with the principle set forth in paragraph 8 of Article 19 of the Constitution of the International Labour Organization the ratification of this Convention by any Member shall not be deemed to affect any existing law, award, custom or agreement in virtue of which members of the armed forces or the police enjoy any right guaranteed by this Convention.

Article 10

In this Convention the term "organization" means any organization of workers or of employers for furthering and defending the interests of workers or of employers.

PART II.　PROTECTION OF THE RIGHT TO ORGANIZE

Article 11

Each Member of the International Labour Organization for which this Convention is in force undertakes to take all necessary and appropriate measures to ensure that workers and employers may exercise freely the right to organize.

Right to Organize and Collective Bargaining Convention, 1949 (No. 98)

Date of entry into force: 18 July 1951

Article 1

1.　Workers shall enjoy adequate protection against acts of anti-union discrimination in respect of their employment.

2. Such protection shall apply more particularly in respect of acts calculated to –

(a) make the employment of a worker subject to the condition that he shall not join a union or shall relinquish trade union membership;

(b) cause the dismissal of or otherwise prejudice a worker by reason of union membership or because of participation in union activities outside working hours or, with the consent of the employer, within working hours.

Article 2

1. Workers' and employers' organizations shall enjoy adequate protection against any acts of interference by each other or each other's agents or members in their establishment, functioning or administration.

2. In particular, acts which are designed to promote the establishment of workers' organizations under the domination of employers' organizations, or to support workers' organizations by financial or other means, with the object of placing such organizations under the control of employers or employers' organizations, shall be deemed to constitute acts of interference within the meaning of this Article.

Article 3

Machinery appropriate to national conditions shall be established, where necessary, for the purpose of ensuring respect for the right to organize as defined in the preceding Articles.

Article 4

Measures appropriate to national conditions shall be taken, where necessary, to encourage and promote the full development and utilization of machinery for voluntary negotiation between employers or employers' organizations and workers' organizations, with a view to the regulation of terms and conditions of employment by means of collective agreements.

Article 5

1. The extent to which the guarantees provided for in this Convention shall apply to the armed forces and the police shall be determined by national laws or regulations.

2. In accordance with the principle set forth in paragraph 8 of article 19 of the Constitution of the International Labour Organization the ratification of this Convention by any Member shall not be deemed to affect any existing law, award, custom or agreement in virtue of which members of the armed forces or the police enjoy any right guaranteed by this Convention.

Article 6

This Convention does not deal with the position of public servants engaged in the administration of the State, nor shall it be construed as prejudicing their rights or status in any way.

Medical Care and Sickness Benefits Convention, 1969 (No. 130)

Date of entry into force: 27 May 1972

PART I.   GENERAL PROVISIONS

Article 1

In this Convention –

(a)   the term "legislation" includes any social security rules as well as laws and regulations;

(b)   the term "prescribed" means determined by or in virtue of national legislation;

(c)   the term "industrial undertaking" includes all undertakings in the following branches of economic activity: mining and quarrying; manufacturing; construction; electricity, gas and water; and transport, storage and communication;

(d)   the term "residence" means ordinary residence in the territory of the Member and the term "resident" means a person ordinarily resident in the territory of the Member;

(e)   the term "dependent" refers to a state of dependency which is presumed to exist in prescribed cases;

(f)   the term "wife" means a wife who is dependent on her husband;

(g)   the term "child" covers –

(i)   a child under school-leaving age or under 15 years of age, whichever is the higher: Provided that a Member which has made a declaration under Article 2 may, while such declaration is in force, apply the Convention as if the term covered a child under school-leaving age or under 15 years of age; and

(ii)   a child under a prescribed age higher than that specified in clause (i) of this subparagraph and who is an apprentice or student or has a chronic illness or infirmity disabling him for any gainful activity, under prescribed conditions: Provided that this requirement shall be deemed to be met where national legislation defines the term so as to cover any child under an age appreciably higher than that specified in clause (i) of this subparagraph;

(h)   the term "standard beneficiary" means a man with a wife and two children;

(i)   the term "qualifying period" means a period of contribution, or a period of employment, or a period of residence, or any combination thereof, as may be prescribed;

(j)   the term "sickness" means any morbid condition, whatever its cause;

(k)   the term "medical care" includes allied benefits.

Article 2

1.   A Member whose economy and medical facilities are insufficiently developed may avail itself, by a declaration accompanying its ratification, of the

temporary exceptions provided for in Article 1, subparagraph (g), clause (1); Article 11; Article 14; Article 20; and Article 26, paragraph 2. Any such declaration shall state the reason for such exceptions.

2.   Each Member which has made a declaration under paragraph 1 of this Article shall include in its reports upon the application of this Convention submitted under article 22 of the Constitution of the International Labour Organization a statement in respect of each exception of which it avails itself –

(a) that its reason for doing so subsists; or

(b) that it renounces its right to avail itself of the exception in question as from a stated date.

3.   Each Member which has made a declaration under paragraph 1 of this Article shall, as appropriate to the terms of such declaration and as circumstances permit –

(a) increase the number of persons protected;

(b) extend the range of medical care provided;

(c) extend the duration of sickness benefit.

Article 3

1.   Any Member whose legislation protects employees may, by a declaration accompanying its ratification, temporarily exclude from the application of this Convention the employees in the sector comprising agricultural occupations who, at the time of the ratification, are not yet protected by legislation which is in conformity with the standards of this Convention.

2.   Each Member which has made a declaration under paragraph 1 of this Article shall indicate in its reports upon the application of this Convention submitted under article 22 of the Constitution of the International Labour Organization to what extent effect is given and what effect is proposed to be given to the provisions of the Convention in respect of the employees in the sector comprising agricultural occupations and any progress which may have been made with a view to the application of the Convention to such employees or, where there is no change to report, shall furnish all the appropriate explanations.

3.   Each Member which has made a declaration under paragraph 1 of this Article shall increase the number of employees protected in the sector comprising agricultural occupations to the extent and with the speed that the circumstances permit.

Article 4

1.   Any Member which ratifies this Convention may, by a declaration accompanying its ratification, exclude from the application of the Convention –

(a) seafarers, including sea fishermen;

(b) public servants;

where these categories are protected by special schemes which provide in the aggregate benefits at least equivalent to those required by this Convention.

2.   Where a declaration under paragraph 1 of this Article is in force, the Member may:

(a) exclude the persons belonging to the category or categories excluded from the application of the Convention from the number of persons taken into account when calculating the percentages specified in Article 5, subparagraph (c); Article 10, subparagraph (b); Article 11; Article 19, subparagraph (b); and Article 20;

(b) exclude the persons belonging to the category or categories excluded from the application of the Convention, as well as the wives and children of such persons, from the number of persons taken into account when calculating the percentage specified in Article 10, subparagraph (c).

3.   Any Member which has made a declaration under paragraph 1 of this Article may subsequently notify the Director-General of the International Labour Office that it accepts the obligations of this Convention in respect of a category or categories excluded at the time of its ratification.

Article 5

Any Member whose legislation protects employees may, as necessary, exclude from the application of this Convention –

(a) persons whose employment is of a casual nature;

(b) members of the employer's family living in his house, in respect of their work for him;

(c) other categories of employees, which shall not exceed in number 10 per cent of all employees other than those excluded under subparagraphs (a) and (b) of this Article.

Article 6

For the purpose of compliance with this Convention, a Member may take account of protection effected by means of insurance which, although not made compulsory by its legislation at the time of ratification for the persons to be protected –

(a) is supervised by the public authorities or administered, in accordance with prescribed standards, by joint operation of employers and workers;

(b) covers a substantial proportion of the persons whose earnings do not exceed those of the skilled manual male employee defined in Article 22, paragraph 6; and

(c) complies, in conjunction with other forms of protection, where appropriate, with the provisions of the Convention.

Article 7

The contingencies covered shall include –

(a) need for medical care of a curative nature and, under prescribed conditions, need for medical care of a preventive nature;

(b) incapacity for work resulting from sickness and involving suspension of earnings, as defined by national legislation.

PART II. MEDICAL CARE
Article 8

Each Member shall secure to the persons protected, subject to prescribed conditions, the provision of medical care of a curative or preventive nature in respect of the contingency referred to in subparagraph (a) of Article 7.

Article 9

The medical care referred to in Article 8 shall be afforded with a view to maintaining, restoring or improving the health of the person protected and his ability to work and to attend to his personal needs.

Article 10

The persons protected in respect of the contingency referred to in subparagraph (a) of Article 7 shall comprise –

(a) all employees, including apprentices, and the wives and children of such employees; or

(b) prescribed classes of the economically active population, constituting not less than 75 per cent of the whole economically active population, and the wives and children of persons in the said classes; or

(c) prescribed classes of residents constituting not less than 75 per cent of all residents.

Article 11

Where a declaration made in virtue of Article 2 is in force, the persons protected in respect of the contingency referred to in subparagraph (a) of Article 7 shall comprise –

(a) prescribed classes of employees, constituting not less than 25 per cent of all employees, and the wives and children of employees in the said classes; or

(b) prescribed classes of employees in industrial undertakings, constituting not less than 50 per cent of all employees in industrial undertakings, and the wives and children of employees in the said classes.

Article 12

Persons who are in receipt of a social security benefit for invalidity, old age, death of the breadwinner or unemployment, and, where appropriate, the wives and children of such persons, shall continue to be protected, under prescribed conditions, in respect of the contingency referred to in subparagraph (a) of Article 7.

Article 13

The medical care referred to in Article 8 shall comprise at least –

(a) general practitioner care, including domiciliary visiting;

(b) specialist care at hospitals for in-patients and out-patients, and such specialist care as may be available outside hospitals;

(c) the necessary pharmaceutical supplies on prescription by medical or other qualified practitioners;

(d) hospitalization where necessary;

(e) dental care, as prescribed; and

(f) medical rehabilitation, including the supply, maintenance and renewal of prosthetic and orthopaedic appliances, as prescribed.

Article 14

Where a declaration made in virtue of Article 2 is in force, the medical care referred to in Article 8 shall comprise at least –

(a) general practitioner care, including, wherever possible, domiciliary visiting;

(b) specialist care at hospitals for in-patients and out-patients, and, wherever possible, such specialist care as may be available outside hospitals;

(c) the necessary pharmaceutical supplies on prescription by medical or other qualified practitioners; and

(d) hospitalization where necessary.

Article 15

Where the legislation of a Member makes the right to the medical care referred to in Article 8 conditional upon the fulfilment of a qualifying period by the person protected or by his breadwinner, the conditions governing the qualifying period shall be such as not to deprive of the right to benefit persons who normally belong to the categories of persons protected.

Article 16

1. The medical care referred to in Article 8 shall be provided throughout the contingency.

2. Where a beneficiary ceases to belong to the categories of persons protected, further entitlement to medical care for a case of sickness which started while he belonged to the said categories may be limited to a prescribed period which shall not be less than 26 weeks: Provided that the medical care shall not cease while the beneficiary continues to receive a sickness benefit.

3. Notwithstanding the provisions of paragraph 2 of this Article, the duration of medical care shall be extended for prescribed diseases recognized as entailing prolonged care.

Article 17

Where the legislation of a Member requires the beneficiary or his breadwinner to share in the cost of the medical care referred to in Article 8, the rules concerning such cost sharing shall be so designed as to avoid hardship and not to prejudice the effectiveness of medical and social protection.

PART III. SICKNESS BENEFIT

Article 18

Each Member shall secure to the persons protected, subject to prescribed conditions, the provisions of sickness benefit in respect of the contingency referred to in subparagraph (b) of Article 7.

Article 19

The persons protected in respect of the contingency specified in subparagraph (b) of Article 7 shall comprise

(a) all employees, including apprentices; or

(b) prescribed classes of the economically active population, constituting not less than 75 per cent of the whole economically active population; or

(c) all residents whose means during the contingency do not exceed limits prescribed in such a manner as to comply with the requirements of Article 24.

Article 20

Where a declaration made in virtue of Article 2 is in force, the persons protected in respect of the contingency referred to in subparagraph (b) of Article 7 shall comprise –

(a) prescribed classes of employees, constituting not less than 25 per cent of all employees; or

(b) prescribed classes of employees in industrial undertakings, constituting not less than 50 per cent of all employees in industrial undertakings.

Article 21

The sickness benefit referred to in Article 18 shall be a periodical payment and shall –

(a) where employees or classes of the economically active population are protected, be calculated in such a manner as to comply either with the requirements of Article 22 or with the requirements of Article 23;

(b) where all residents whose means during the contingency do not exceed prescribed limits are protected, be calculated in such a manner as to comply with the requirements of Article 24.

Article 22

1. In the case of a periodical payment to which this Article applies, the rate of the benefit, increased by the amount of any family allowances payable during the contingency, shall be such as to attain for the standard beneficiary, in respect of the contingency referred to in subparagraph (b) of Article 7, at least 60 per cent of the total of the previous earnings of the beneficiary and of the amount of any family allowances payable to a person protected with the same family responsibilities as the standard beneficiary.

2. The previous earnings of the beneficiary shall be calculated according to prescribed rules, and, where the persons protected are arranged in classes according to their earnings, their previous earnings may be calculated from the basic earnings of the classes to which they belonged.

3. A maximum limit may be prescribed for the rate of the benefit or for the earnings taken into account for the calculation of the benefit, provided that the maximum limit is fixed in such a way that the provisions of paragraph 1 of this

Article are complied with where the previous earnings of the beneficiary are equal to or lower than the wage of a skilled manual male employee.

4.   The previous earnings of the beneficiary, the wage of the skilled manual male employee, the benefit and any family allowances shall be calculated on the same time basis.

5.   For the other beneficiaries the benefit shall bear a reasonable relation to the benefit for the standard beneficiary.

6.   For the purpose of this Article, a skilled manual male employee shall be –

(a)   a fitter or turner in the manufacture of machinery other than electrical machinery; or

(b)   a person deemed typical of skilled labour selected in accordance with the provisions of the following paragraph; or

(c)   a person whose earnings are such as to be equal to or greater than the earnings of 75 per cent of all the persons protected, such earnings to be determined on the basis of annual or shorter periods as may be prescribed; or

(d)   a person whose earnings are equal to 125 per cent of the average earnings of all the persons protected.

7.   The person deemed typical of skilled labour for the purposes of subparagraph (b) of the preceding paragraph shall be a person employed in the major group of economic activities with the largest number of economically active male persons protected in the contingency referred to in subparagraph (b) of Article 7 in the division comprising the largest number of such persons; for this purpose, the International Standard Industrial Classification of All Economic Activities adopted by the Economic and Social Council of the United Nations at its Seventh Session on 27 August 1948, as amended up to 1968 and reproduced in the Annex to this Convention, or such classification as at any time further amended, shall be used.

8.   Where the rate of benefit varies by region, the skilled manual male employee may be determined for each region in accordance with paragraphs 6 and 7 of this Article.

9.   The wage of the skilled manual male employee shall be determined on the basis of the rates of wages for normal hours of work fixed by collective agreements, by or in pursuance of national legislation, where applicable, or by custom, including cost-of-living allowances if any; where such rates differ by region but paragraph 8 of this Article is not applied, the median rate shall be taken.

Article 23

1.   In the case of a periodical payment to which this Article applies, the rate of the benefit, increased by the amount of any family allowances payable during the contingency, shall be such as to attain for the standard beneficiary, in respect of the contingency referred to in subparagraph (b) of Article 7, at least 60 per cent of the total of the wage of an ordinary adult male labourer and of the amount of

any family allowances payable to a person protected with the same family responsibilities as the standard beneficiary.

2.   The wage of the ordinary adult male labourer, the benefit and any family allowances shall be calculated on the same time basis.

3.   For the other beneficiaries, the benefit shall bear a reasonable relation to the benefit for the standard beneficiary.

4.   For the purpose of this Article, the ordinary adult male labourer shall be –

(a) a person deemed typical of unskilled labour in the manufacture of machinery other than electrical machinery; or

(b) a person deemed typical of unskilled labour selected in accordance with the provisions of the following paragraph.

5.   The person deemed typical of unskilled labour for the purpose of subparagraph (b) of the preceding paragraph shall be a person employed in the major group of economic activities with the largest number of economically active male persons protected in the contingency referred to in subparagraph (b) of Article 7 in the division comprising the largest number of such persons; for this purpose, the International Standard Industrial Classification of All Economic Activities adopted by the Economic and Social Council of the United Nations at its Seventh Session on 27 August 1948, as amended up to 1968 and reproduced in the Annex to this Convention, or such classification as at any time further amended, shall be used.

6.   Where the rate of benefit varies by region, the ordinary adult male labourer may be determined for each region in accordance with paragraphs 4 and 5 of this Article.

7.   The wage of the ordinary adult male labourer shall be determined on the basis of the rates of wages for normal hours of work fixed by collective agreements, by or in pursuance of national legislation, where applicable, or by custom, including cost-of-living allowances, if any; where such rates differ by region but paragraph 6 of this Article is not applied, the median rate shall be taken.

Article 24

In the case of a periodical payment to which this Article applies –

(a) the rate of the benefit shall be determined according to a prescribed scale or a scale fixed by the competent public authority in conformity with prescribed rules;

(b) such rate may be reduced only to the extent by which the other means of the family of the beneficiary exceed prescribed substantial amounts or substantial amounts fixed by the competent public authority in conformity with prescribed rules;

(c) the total of the benefit and any other means, after deduction of the substantial amounts referred to in subparagraph (b), shall be sufficient to maintain the family of the beneficiary in health and decency, and shall be not less than the corresponding benefit calculated in accordance with the requirements of Article 23;

(d) the provisions of subparagraph (c) shall be deemed to be satisfied if the total amount of sickness benefits paid under this Convention exceeds by at least 30 per cent the total amount of benefits which would be obtained by applying the provisions of Article 23 and the provisions of subparagraph (b) of Article 19.

Article 25

Where the legislation of a Member makes the right to the sickness benefit referred to in Article 18 conditional upon the fulfilment of a qualifying period by the person protected, the conditions governing the qualifying period shall be such as not to deprive of the right to benefit persons who normally belong to the categories of persons protected.

Article 26

1. The sickness benefit referred to in Article 18 shall be granted throughout the contingency: Provided that the grant of benefit may be limited to not less than 52 weeks in each case of incapacity, as prescribed.

2. Where a declaration made in virtue of Article 2 is in force, the grant of the sickness benefit referred to in Article 18 may be limited to not less than 26 weeks in each case of incapacity, as prescribed.

3. Where the legislation of a Member provides that sickness benefit is not payable for an initial period of suspension of earnings, such period shall not exceed three days.

Article 27

1. In the case of the death of a person who was in receipt of, or qualified for, the sickness benefit referred to in Article 18, a funeral benefit shall, under prescribed conditions, be paid to his survivors, to any other dependants or to the person who has borne the expense of the funeral.

2. A member may derogate from the provision of paragraph 1 of this Article where –

(a) it has accepted the obligations of Part IV of the Invalidity Old-Age and Survivors' Benefits Convention, 1967;

(b) it provides in its legislation for cash sickness benefit at a rate of not less than 80 per cent of the earnings of the persons protected; and

(c) the majority of persons protected are covered by voluntary insurance which is supervised by the public authorities and which provides a funeral grant.

PART IV. COMMON PROVISIONS

Article 28

1. A benefit to which a person protected would otherwise be entitled in compliance with this Convention may be suspended to such extent as may be prescribed –

(a) as long as the person concerned is absent from the territory of the Member;

(b) as long as the person concerned is being indemnified for the contingency by a third party to the extent of the indemnity;

(c) where the person concerned has made a fraudulent claim;

(d) where the contingency has been caused by a criminal offence committed by the person concerned;

(e) where the contingency has been caused by the serious and wilful misconduct of the person concerned;

(f) where the person concerned, without good cause, neglects to make use of the medical care or the rehabilitation services placed at his disposal, or fails to comply with rules prescribed for verifying the occurrence or continuance of the contingency or for the conduct of beneficiaries;

(g) in the case of the sickness benefit referred to in Article 18, as long as the person concerned is maintained at public expense or at the expense of a social security institution or service; and

(h) in the case of the sickness benefit referred to in Article 18, as long as the person concerned is in receipt of another social security cash benefit, other than a family benefit, subject to the part of the benefit which is suspended not exceeding the other benefit.

2. In the cases and within the limits prescribed, part of the benefit otherwise due shall be paid to the dependants of the person concerned.

Article 29

1. Every claimant shall have a right of appeal in the case of refusal of the benefit or complaint as to its quality or quantity.

2. Where in the application of this Convention a government department responsible to a legislature is entrusted with the administration of medical care, the right of appeal provided for in paragraph 1 of this Article may be replaced by a right to have a complaint concerning the refusal of medical care or the quality of the care received investigated by the appropriate authority.

Article 30

1. Each Member shall accept general responsibility for the due provision of the benefits provided in compliance with this Convention and shall take all measures required for this purpose.

2. Each Member shall accept general responsibility for the proper administration of the institutions and services concerned in the application of this Convention.

Article 31

Where the administration is not entrusted to an institution regulated by the public authorities or to a government department responsible to a legislature –

(a) representatives of the persons protected shall participate in the management under prescribed conditions;

(b) national legislation shall, where appropriate, provide for the participation of representatives of employers;

(c) national legislation may likewise decide as to the participation of representatives of the public authorities.

Article 32

Each Member shall, within its territory, assure to non-nationals who normally reside or work there equality of treatment with its own nationals as regards the right to the benefits provided for in this Convention.

Article 33

1.   A Member –

(a) which has accepted the obligations of this Convention without availing itself of the exceptions and exclusions provided for in Article 2 and Article 3;

(b) which provides overall higher benefits than those provided in this Convention and whose total relevant expenditure on medical care and sickness benefits amounts to at least 4 per cent of its national income; and

(c) which satisfies at least two of the three following conditions:

   (i)   it covers a percentage of the economically active population which is at least ten points higher than the percentage required by Article 10, paragraph (b), and by Article 19, subparagraph (b), or a percentage of all residents which is at least ten points higher than the percentage required by Article 10, subparagraph (c);

   (ii) it provides medical care of a curative and preventive nature of an appreciably higher standard than that prescribed by Article 13;

   (iii) it provides sickness benefit corresponding to a percentage at least ten points higher than is required by Articles 22 and 23;

   may, after consultation with the most representative organizations of employers and workers, where such exist, make temporary derogations from particular provisions of Parts II and III of this Convention on condition that such derogation shall neither fundamentally reduce nor impair the essential guarantees of this Convention.

2.   Each Member which has made such a derogation shall indicate in its reports upon the application of this Convention submitted under article 22 of the Constitution of the International Labour Organization the position of its law and practice as regards such derogation and any progress made towards complete application of the terms of the Convention.

Article 34

This Convention shall not apply to –

(a) contingencies which occurred before the coming into force of the Convention for the Member concerned;

(b) benefits in contingencies occurring after the coming into force of the Convention for the Member concerned in so far as the rights to such benefits are derived from periods preceding that date.

PART V. FINAL PROVISIONS

Article 35

This Convention revises the Sickness Insurance (Industry) Convention, 1927, and the Sickness Insurance (Agriculture) Convention, 1927.

Article 36

1. In conformity with the provisions of Article 75 of the Social Security (Minimum Standards) Convention, 1952, Part III of that Convention and the relevant provisions of other Parts thereof shall cease to apply to any Member having ratified this Convention as from the date at which this Convention is binding on that Member and no declaration under Article 3 is in force.

2. Acceptance of the obligations of this Convention shall, on condition that no declaration under Article 3 is in force, be deemed to constitute acceptance of the obligations of Part III of the Social Security (Minimum Standards) Convention, 1952, and the relevant provisions of other Parts thereof, for the purpose of Article 2 of the said Convention.

Article 37

If any Convention which may be adopted subsequently by the Conference concerning any subject or subjects dealt with in this Convention so provides, such provisions of this Convention as may be specified in the said Convention shall cease to apply to any Member having ratified the said Convention as from the date at which the said Convention comes into force for that Member.

Annex

International Standard Industrial Classification of All Economic Activities
(Revised up to 1968)

LIST OF MAJOR DIVISIONS, DIVISIONS AND MAJOR GROUPS

Division	Major Group	
		Major Division 1. Agriculture, Hunting, Forestry and Fishing
11		Agriculture and Hunting
	111	Agricultural and livestock production
	112	Agricultural services
	113	Hunting, trapping and game propagation
12		Forestry and Logging
	121	Forestry
	122	Logging
13	130	Fishing
21	210	Coal Mining

Division	Major Group	

Major Division 2. Mining and Quarrying

22	220	Crude Petroleum and Natural Gas Production
23	230	Metal Ore Mining
29	290	Other Mining

Major Division 3. Manufacturing

31		Manufacture of Food, Beverages and Tobacco
	311-312	Food manufacturing
	313	Beverage industries
	314	Tobacco manufactures
32		Textile, Wearing Apparel and Leather Industries
	321	Manufacture of textiles
	322	Manufacture of wearing apparel, except footwear
	323	Manufacture of leather and products of leather, leather substitutes and fur, except footwear and wearing apparel
	324	Manufacture of footwear, except vulcanized or moulded rubber or plastic footwear
33		Manufacture of Wood and Wood Products, Including Furniture
	331	Manufacture of wood and wood and cork products, except furniture
	332	Manufacture of furniture and fixtures, except primarily of metal
34		Manufacture of Paper and Paper Products, Printing and Publishing
	341	Manufacture of paper and paper products
	342	Printing, publishing and allied industries
35		Manufacture of Chemicals and Chemical, Petroleum, Coal, Rubber and Plastic Products
	351	Manufacture of industrial chemicals
	352	Manufacture of other chemical products
	353	Petroleum refineries
	354	Manufacture of miscellaneous products of petroleum and coal
	355	Manufacture of rubber products
	356	Manufacture of plastic products not elsewhere classified
36		Manufacture of Non-Metallic Mineral Products, except Products of Petroleum and Coal
	361	Manufacture of pottery, china and earthenware
	362	Manufacture of glass and glass products
	369	Manufacture of other non-metallic mineral products
37		Basic Metal Industries
	371	Iron and steel basic industries
	372	Non-ferrous metal basic industries
38		Manufacture of Fabricated Metal Products, Machinery and Equipment
	381	Manufacture of fabricated metal products, except machinery and equipment
	382	Manufacture of machinery except electrical
	383	Manufacture of electrical machinery apparatus, appliances and supplies
	384	Manufacture of transport equipment
	385	Manufacture of professional and scientific and measuring and controlling equipment not elsewhere classified, and of photographic and optical goods
39	390	Other Manufacturing Industries

Major Division 4. Electricity, Gas and Water

| 41 | 410 | Electricity, Gas and Steam |
| 42 | 420 | Water Works and Supply |

Division	Major Group	

Minimum Age Convention, 1973 (No. 138)

Date of entry into force: 19 June 1976

Article 1

Each Member for which this Convention is in force undertakes to pursue a national policy designed to ensure the effective abolition of child labour and to raise progressively the minimum age for admission to employment or work to a level consistent with the fullest physical and mental development of young persons.

Article 2

1.   Each Member which ratifies this Convention shall specify, in a declaration appended to its ratification, a minimum age for admission to employment or work within its territory and on means of transport registered in its territory; subject to Articles 4 to 8 of this Convention, no one under that age shall be admitted to employment or work in any occupation.

2.   Each Member which has ratified this Convention may subsequently notify the Director-General of the International Labour Office, by further declarations, that it specifies a minimum age higher than that previously specified.

3.   The minimum age specified in pursuance of paragraph 1 of this Article shall not be less than the age of completion of compulsory schooling and, in any case, shall not be less than 15 years.

4.   Notwithstanding the provisions of paragraph 3 of this Article, a Member whose economy and educational facilities are insufficiently developed may, after consultation with the organizations of employers and workers concerned, where such exist, initially specify a minimum age of 14 years.

5.   Each Member which has specified a minimum age of 14 years in pursuance of the provisions of the preceding paragraph shall include in its reports on the application of this Convention submitted under article 22 of the Constitution of the International Labour Organization a statement –

(a)   that its reason for doing so subsists; or

(b)   that it renounces its right to avail itself of the provisions in question as from a stated date.

Article 3

1.   The minimum age for admission to any type of employment or work which by its nature or the circumstances in which it is carried out is likely to jeopardize the health, safety or morals of young persons shall not be less than 18 years.

2.   The types of employment or work to which paragraph 1 of this Article applies shall be determined by national laws or regulations or by the competent authority, after consultation with the organizations of employers and workers concerned, where such exist.

3.   Notwithstanding the provisions of paragraph 1 of this Article, national laws or regulations or the competent authority may, after consultation with the organizations of employers and workers concerned, where such exist, authorize

employment or work as from the age of 16 years on condition that the health, safety and morals of the young persons concerned are fully protected and that the young persons have received adequate specific instruction or vocational training in the relevant branch of activity.

Article 4

1. In so far as necessary, the competent authority, after consultation with the organizations of employers and workers concerned, where such exist, may exclude from the application of this Convention limited categories of employment or work in respect of which special and substantial problems of application arise.

2. Each Member which ratifies this Convention shall list in its first report on the application of the Convention submitted under article 22 of the Constitution of the International Labour Organization any categories which may have been excluded in pursuance of paragraph 1 of this Article, giving the reasons for such exclusion, and shall state in subsequent reports the position of its law and practice in respect of the categories excluded and the extent to which effect has been given or is proposed to be given to the Convention in respect of such categories.

3. Employment or work covered by Article 3 of this Convention shall not be excluded from the application of the Convention in pursuance of this Article.

Article 5

1. A Member whose economy and administrative facilities are insufficiently developed may, after consultation with the organizations of employers and workers concerned, where such exist, initially limit the scope of application of this Convention.

2. Each Member which avails itself of the provisions of paragraph 1 of this Article shall specify, in a declaration appended to its ratification, the branches of economic activity or types of undertakings to which it will apply the provisions of the Convention.

3. The provisions of the Convention shall be applicable as a minimum to the following: mining and quarrying; manufacturing; construction; electricity, gas and water; sanitary services; transport, storage and communication; and plantations and other agricultural undertakings mainly producing for commercial purposes, but excluding family and small-scale holdings producing for local consumption and not regularly employing hired workers.

4. Any Member which has limited the scope of application of this Convention in pursuance of this Article –

(a) shall indicate in its reports under article 22 of the Constitution of the International Labour Organization the general position as regards the employment or work of young persons and children in the branches of activity which are excluded from the scope of application of this Convention and any progress which may have been made towards wider application of the provisions of the Convention;

(b) may at any time formally extend the scope of application by a declaration addressed to the Director-General of the International Labour Office.

Article 6

This Convention does not apply to work done by children and young persons in schools for general, vocational or technical education or in other training institutions, or to work done by persons at least 14 years of age in undertakings, where such work is carried out in accordance with conditions prescribed by the competent authority, after consultation with the organizations of employers and workers concerned, where such exist, and is an integral part of –

(a) a course of education or training for which a school or training institution is primarily responsible;

(b) a programme of training mainly or entirely in an undertaking, which programme has been approved by the competent authority; or

(c) a programme of guidance or orientation designed to facilitate the choice of an occupation or of a line of training.

Article 7

1. National laws or regulations may permit the employment or work of persons 13 to 15 years of age on light work which is –

(a) not likely to be harmful to their health or development; and

(b) not such as to prejudice their attendance at school, their participation in vocational orientation or training programmes approved by the competent authority or their capacity to benefit from the instruction received.

2. National laws or regulations may also permit the employment or work of persons who are at least 15 years of age but have not yet completed their compulsory schooling on work which meets the requirements set forth in subparagraphs (a) and (b) of paragraph 1 of this Article.

3. The competent authority shall determine the activities in which employment or work may be permitted under paragraphs 1 and 2 of this Article and shall prescribe the number of hours during which and the conditions in which such employment or work may be undertaken.

4. Notwithstanding the provisions of paragraphs 1 and 2 of this Article, a Member which has availed itself of the provisions of paragraph 4 of Article 2 may, for as long as it continues to do so, substitute the ages 12 and 14 for the ages 13 and 15 in paragraph 1 and the age 14 for the age 15 in paragraph 2 of this Article.

Article 8

1. After consultation with the organizations of employers and workers concerned, where such exist the competent authority may, by permits granted in individual cases, allow exceptions to the prohibition of employment or work provided for in Article 2 of this Convention, for such purposes as participation in artistic performances.

2. Permits so granted shall limit the number of hours during which and prescribe the conditions in which employment or work is allowed.

Article 9

1. All necessary measures, including the provision of appropriate penalties, shall be taken by the competent authority to ensure the effective enforcement of the provision of this Convention.

2. National laws or regulations or the competent authority shall define the persons responsible for compliance with the provisions giving effect to the Convention.

3. National laws or regulations or the competent authority shall prescribe the registers or other documents which shall be kept and made available by the employer; such registers or documents shall contain the names and ages or dates of birth, duly certified wherever possible, of persons whom he employs or who work for him and who are less than 18 years of age.

Article 10

1. This Convention revises, on the terms set forth in this Article, the Minimum Age (Industry) Convention, 1919, the Minimum Age (Sea) Convention, 1920, the Minimum Age (Agriculture) Convention, 1921, the Minimum Age (Trimmers and Stokers) Convention, 1921, the Minimum Age (Non-Industrial Employment) Convention, 1932, the Minimum Age (Sea) Convention (Revised), 1936, the Minimum Age (Industry) Convention (Revised), 1937, the Minimum Age (Non-Industrial Employment) Convention (Revised), 1937, the Minimum Age (Fishermen) Convention, 1959, and the Minimum Age (Underground Work) Convention, 1965.

2. The coming into force of this Convention shall not close the Minimum Age (Sea) Convention (Revised), 1936, the Minimum Age (Industry) Convention (Revised), 1937, the Minimum Age (Non-Industrial Employment) Convention (Revised), 1937, the Minimum Age (Fishermen) Convention, 1959, or the Minimum Age (Underground Work) Convention, 1965, to further ratification.

3. The Minimum Age (Industry) Convention, 1919, the Minimum Age (Sea) Convention, 1920, the Minimum Age (Agriculture) Convention 1921, and the Minimum Age (Trimmers and Stokers) Convention, 1921, shall be closed to further ratification when all the parties thereto have consented to such closing by ratification of this Convention or by a declaration communicated to the Director-General of the International Labour Office.

4. When the obligations of this Convention are accepted –

(a) by a Member which is a party to the Minimum Age (Industry) Convention (Revised), 1937, and a minimum age of not less than 15 years is specified in pursuance of Article 2 of this Convention, this shall *ipso jure* involve the immediate denunciation of that Convention;

(b) in respect of non-industrial employment as defined in the Minimum Age (Non-Industrial Employment) Convention, 1932, by a Member which is a party to that Convention, this shall *ipso jure* involve the immediate denunciation of that Convention;

(c) in respect of non-industrial employment as defined in the Minimum Age (Non-Industrial Employment) Convention (Revised), 1937, by a Member which is a party to that Convention, and a minimum age of not less than 15 years is specified in pursuance of Article 2 of this Convention, this shall *ipso jure* involve the immediate denunciation of that Convention;

(d) in respect of maritime employment, by a Member which is a party to the Minimum Age (Sea) Convention (Revised), 1936, and a minimum age of not less than 15 years is specified in pursuance of Article 2 of this Convention or the Member specifies that Article 3 of this Convention applies to maritime employment, this shall *ipso jure* involve the immediate denunciation of that Convention;

(e) in respect of employment in maritime fishing, by a Member which is a party to the Minimum Age (Fishermen) Convention, 1959, and a minimum age of not less than 15 years is specified in pursuance of Article 2 of this Convention or the Member specifies that Article 3 of this Convention applies to employment in maritime fishing, this shall *ipso jure* involve the immediate denunciation of that Convention;

(f) by a Member which is a party to the Minimum Age (Underground Work) Convention, 1965, and a minimum age of not less than the age specified in pursuance of that Convention is specified in pursuance of Article 2 of this Convention or the Member specifies that such an age applies to employment underground in mines in virtue of Article 3 of this Convention, this shall *ipso jure* involve the immediate denunciation of that Convention, if and when this Convention shall have come into force.

5. Acceptance of the obligations of this Convention –

(a) shall involve the denunciation of the Minimum Age (Industry) Convention, 1919, in accordance with Article 12 thereof;

(b) in respect of agriculture shall involve the denunciation of the Minimum Age (Agriculture) Convention, 1921, in accordance with Article 9 thereof;

(c) in respect of maritime employment shall involve the denunciation of the Minimum Age (Sea) Convention, 1920, in accordance with Article 10 thereof, and of the Minimum Age (Trimmers and Stokers) Convention, 1921, in accordance with Article 12 thereof, if and when this Convention shall have come into force.

MARITIME LABOUR CONVENTIONS

No.		No. of ratifications as at 26 Dec. 1993
7	Minimum Age (Sea) Convention, 1920	50
8	Unemployment Indemnity Shipwreck Convention, 1920	57
9	Placing of Seamen Convention, 1920	37
15	Minimum Age (Trimmers and Stokers) Convention, 1921	67
16	Medical Examination of Young Persons (Sea) Convention, 1921	76
22	Seamen's Articles of Agreement Convention, 1926	56
23	Repatriation of Seamen Convention, 1926	43
53	Officers' Competency Certificates Convention, 1936	32
54 *	Holidays with Pay (Sea) Convention, 1936	6
55	Shipowners' Liability (Sick and Injured Seamen) Convention, 1936	16
56 +	Sickness Insurance (Sea) Convention, 1936	18
57 *	Hours of Work and Manning (Sea) Convention, 1936	4
58	Minimum Age (Sea) Convention (Revised), 1936	50
68	Food and Catering (Ships' Crews) Convention, 1946	22
69	Certification of Ships' Cooks Convention, 1946	34
70 *	Social Security (Seafarers) Convention, 1946	7
71	Seafarers' Pensions Convention, 1946	13
72 *	Paid Vacations (Seafarers) Convention, 1946	5
73	Medical Examination (Seafarers) Convention, 1946	40
74	Certification of Able Seamen Convention, 1946	26
75 *	Accommodation of Crews Convention, 1946	5
76 *	Wages, Hours of Work and Manning (Sea) Convention, 1946	1
91 +	Paid Vacations (Seafarers) Convention (Revised), 1949	23
92	Accommodation of Crews Convention (Revised), 1949	39
93 *	Wages, Hours of Work and Manning (Sea) Convention (Revised), 1949	6
108	Seafarers' Identity Documents Convention, 1958	52
109 *	Wages, Hours of Work and Manning (Sea) Convention (Revised), 1958	15
133	Accommodation of Crews (Supplementary Provisions) Convention, 1970	25
134	Prevention of Accidents (Seafarers) Convention, 1970	26
145	Continuity of Employment (Seafarers) Convention, 1976	17
146	Seafarers' Annual Leave with Pay Convention, 1976	12

* Conventions which did not receive the requisite number of ratifications.
+ Conventions included in this volume which are closed to ratification.

Maritime labour Conventions and Recommendations

No.		No. of ratifications as at 26 Dec. 1993
147	Merchant Shipping (Minimum Standards) Convention, 1976	29
163	Seafarers' Welfare at Sea and in Port Convention, 1987	10
164	Health Protection and Medical Care of Seafarers Convention, 1987	6
165	Social Security for Seafarers Convention (Revised), 1987	2
166	Repatriation of Seafarers Convention (Revised), 1987	4
Total		**953**

MARITIME LABOUR RECOMMENDATIONS

No.	
9	National Seamen's Codes Recommendation, 1920
10	Unemployment Insurance (Seamen) Recommendation, 1920
27	Repatriation (Ship Masters and Apprentices) Recommendation, 1926
28	Labour Inspection (Seamen) Recommendation, 1926
48	Seamen's Welfare in Ports Recommendation, 1936
49	Hours of Work and Manning (Sea) Recommendation, 1936
75	Seafarers' Social Security (Agreements) Recommendation, 1946
76	Seafarers' (Medical Care for Dependants) Recommendation, 1946
77	Vocational Training (Seafarers) Recommendation, 1946
78	Bedding, Mess Utensils and Miscellaneous Provisions (Ships' Crews) Recommendation, 1946
105	Ships' Medicine Chests Recommendation, 1958
106	Medical Advice at Sea Recommendation, 1958
107	Seafarers' Engagement (Foreign Vessels) Recommendation, 1958
108	Social Conditions and Safety (Seafarers) Recommendation, 1958
109	Wages, Hours of Work and Manning (Sea) Recommendation, 1958
137	Vocational Training (Seafarers) Recommendation, 1970
138	Seafarers' Welfare Recommendation, 1970
139	Employment of Seafarers (Technical Developments) Recommendation, 1970
140	Crew Accommodation (Air Conditioning) Recommendation, 1970
141	Crew Accommodation (Noise Control) Recommendation, 1970
142	Prevention of Accidents (Seafarers) Recommendation, 1970
153	Protection of Young Seafarers Recommendation, 1976
154	Continuity of Employment (Seafarers) Recommendation, 1976
155	Merchant Shipping (Improvement of Standards) Recommendation, 1976
173	Seafarers' Welfare Recommendation, 1987
174	Repatriation of Seafarers Recommendation, 1987

CHART OF RATIFICATIONS OF MARITIME
AND OTHER INTERNATIONAL LABOUR CONVENTIONS
REFERRED TO IN THIS VOLUME[1]
(as at 14 December 1993)

Albania	16, 58, 87, 98
Algeria	56, (58), 68, 69, (70), 71, (72), 73, 74, 87, 91, 92, 98, 108, 138
Angola	7, 68, 69, 73, 74, 91, 92, 98, 108
Antigua and Barbuda	87, 98, 108, 138
Argentina	7, 8, 9, 15, 16, 22, 23, 53, 58, 68, 71, 73, 87, 98
Australia	7, 8, 9, 15, 16, 22, (57), 58, (76), 87, 92, (93), 98, (109), 133
Austria	87, 98
Azerbaijan	16, 23, 69, 73, 87, 92, 98, 108, 133, 134, 138, 147
Bahamas	7, 22, 98
Bangladesh	15, 16, 22, 87, 98
Barbados	7, 22, 74, 87, 98, 108
Belarus	(15), 16, (58), 87, 98, 138
Belgium	7, 8, 9, (15), 16, 22, 23, 53, (54), 55, 56, (57), (58), 68, 69, 73, 74, 87, 91, 92, 98, 138, 147
Belize	7, 8, 15, 16, 22, 58, 87, 98, 108
Benin	87, 98
Bolivia	87, 98, 130
Bosnia and Herzegovina	8, 9, 16, 22, 23, 53, 56, 69, 73, 74, 87, 91, 92, 98, (109), 138
Brazil	(7), 16, 22, 53, 58, 91, 92, (93), 98, 108, (109), 133, 145, 147
Bulgaria	(7), 8, 9, (15), 16, 22, 23, 53, (54), 55, 56, (57), (58), 68, 69, 71, (72), 73, (75), 87, 98, 108, 138
Burkino Faso	87, 98
Burundi	87,
Cameroon	9, 15, 16, 87, 98, 108, 146
Canada	7, 8, 15, 16, 22, 58, 68, 69, 73, 74, 87, 108, 147
Cape Verde	98
Central African Republic	87, 98
Chad	87, 98
Chile	7, 8, 9, 15, 16, 22
China	7, 15, 16, 22, 23

[1]Numbers in parentheses denote Conventions ratified but not in force for the country concerned.

Colombia	7, 8, 9, 15, 16, 22, 23, 87, 98
Comoros	87, 98
Congo	87
Costa Rica	8, 16, 87, 92, 98, 130, 134, 138, 145, 147
Côte d'Ivoire	87, 98, 133
Croatia	8, 9, 16, 22, 23, 53, 56, 69, 73, 74, 87, 91, 92, 98, (109), 138
Cuba	(7), 8, 9, (15), 16, 22, 23, 53, (58), (72), 87, 91, 92, (93), 98, 108, 138, 145
Cyprus	15, 16, 87, 98
Czech Republic	87, 98, 130, 163, 164
Denmark	7, 8, 9, 15, 16, 53, 58, 73, 87, 92, 98, 108, 130, 134, 147, 163
Djibouti	9, 15, 16, 22, 23, 53, 55, 56, 58, 69, 71, 73, 87, 91, 98, 108
Dominica	8, 16, 22, 87, 98, 108, 138
Dominican Republic	7, 87, 98
Ecuador	87, 98, 130
Egypt	9, 22, 23, 53, 55, 56, 68, 69, 71, 73, 74, 87, 92, 98, 134, 145, 147
Equatorial Guinea	138
Estonia	7, 8, 9, 15, 16, 22, 23, 53
Ethiopia	87, 98
Fiji	8, 58, 98, 108
Finland	(7), 8, 9, (15), 16, 22, 53, (72), 73, (75), 87, (91), 92, 98, 108, 130, 133, 134, 138, 145, 146, 147, 163
France	8, 9, (15), 16, 22, 23, 53, (54), 55, 56, (58), 68, 69, (70), 71, (72), 73, 74, (75), 87, (91), 92, 98, 108, (109), 133, 134, 138, 145, 146, 147
Gabon	87, 98
Germany	(7), 8, 9, (15), 16, 22, 23, 53, 56, 73, 87, 92, 98, 130, 133, 134, 138, 147
Ghana	8, 15, 16, 22, 23, 58, 69, 74, 87, 92, 98, 108
Greece	(7), 8, 9, (15), 16, 23, 55, (58), 68, 69, 71, 73, 87, 92, 98, 108, 133, 134, 138, 147
Grenada	7, 8, 15, 16, 58, 98, 108
Guatemala	(15), 16, 58, 87, 98, 108, (109), 138
Guinea	16, 87, 98, 133, 134
Guinea-Bissau	7, 68, 69, 73, 74, 91, 92, 98, 108
Guyana	7, 15, 87, 98, 108
Haiti	87, 98
Honduras	87, 98, 108, 138
Hungary	7, 15, 16, 87, 98, 145, 163, 164, 165, 166
Iceland	15, 58, 87, 91, 98, 108
India	15, 16, 22
Indonesia	69, 98
Iran, Islamic Republic of	108
Iraq	8, (15), 16, 22, 23, (58), 92, (93), 98, 108, (109), 138, 145, 146, 147

Ireland	(7), 8, (15), 16, 22, 23, 53, 68, 69, 73, 74, 87, 92, 98, 108, 138, 147
Israel	9, 53, 87, 91, 92, 98, 133, 134, 138
Italy	(7), 8, 9, (15), 16, 22, 23, 53, 55, (58), 68, 69, 71, 73, 74, 87, (91), 92, 98, 108, (109), 133, 134, 138, 145, 146, 147
Jamaica	7, 8, 15, 16, 58, 87, 98
Japan	7, 8, 9, 15, 16, 22, 58, 69, 73, 87, 98, 134, 147
Jordan	98
Kenya	(15), 16, (58), 98, 134, 138, 146
Korea, Republic of	73
Kuwait	87
Kyrgyzstan	16, 23, 69, 73, 87, 92, 98, 108, 133, 134, 138, 147
Latvia	87, 98, 108
Lebanon	8, 9, 15, 58, 71, 73, 74, 98, (109), 133, 147
Lesotho	87, 98
Liberia	22, 23, 53, 55, 58, 87, 92, 98, 108, 133, 147
Libyan Arab Jamahiriya	53, 98, 130, 138
Luxembourg	(7), 8, 9, (15), 16, 22, (23), 53, 55, 56, 68, 69, 73, 74, 87, 92, 98, 108, 130, 138, 147, 166
Madagascar	87
Malawi	98
Malaysia	98
Mali	87, 98
Malta	(7), 8, (15), 16, 22, 73, 87, 98, 108, 138
Mauritania	15, 22, 23, 53, 58, 87, 91
Mauritius	(7), 8, (15), 16, (58), 74, 98, 108, 138
Mexico	(7), 8, 9, 16, 22, 23, 53, 54, 55, 56, 58, 87, 108, (109), 134, 163, 164, 166
Mongolia	87, 98
Morocco	15, 22, 55, 98, 145, 146, 147
Myanmar	15, 16, 22, 87
Netherlands	(7), 8, 9, (15), 16, 22, 23, (58), 68, 69, (70), 71, 73, 74, 87, (91), 92, 98, 133, 138, 145, 146, 147
New Zealand	8, 9, 15, 16, 22, 23, 53, 58, 68, 69, 74, 92, 133, 134, 145
Nicaragua	(7), 8, 9, (15), 16, 22, 23, 87, 98, 138, 146
Niger	87, 98, 138
Nigeria	8, 15, 16, 58, 87, 98, 133, 134
Norway	(7), 8, 9, (15), 16, 22, 53, 56, (58), 68, 69, 71, 73, (75), 87, 91, 92, 98, 108, (109), 130, 133, 134, 138, 145, 147, 163
Pakistan	15, 16, 22, 87, 98
Panama	8, 9, 15, 16, 22, 23, 53, 55, 56, 58, 68, 69, 71, 73, 74, 87, 92, 98, 108
Papua New Guinea	7, 8, 22, 98
Paraguay	87, 98
Peru	8, 9, 22, 23, 53, 55, 56, 58, 68, 69, (70), 71, 73, 87, 98
Philippines	23, 53, 87, (93), 98

Poland	(7), 8, 9, (15), 16, 22, 23, 68, 69, (70), 73, 74, 87, 91, 92, 98, 108, 133, 134, 138, 145
Portugal	7, 8, 22, 23, 68, 69, 73, 74, 87, (91), 92, 98, 108, (109), 145, 146, 147
Romania	(7), 8, 9, (15), 16, 87, 98, 108, 134, 138
Russian Federation	(15), 16, 23, (58), 69, 73, 87, 92, 98, 108, 133, 134, 138, 147
Rwanda	87, 98, 138
Saint Lucia	7, 8, 15, 16, 87, 98, 108
San Marino	87, 98
Sao Tome and Principe	87, 98
Senegal	87, 98
Seychelles	7, 8, 15, 16, 58, 87, 108
Sierra Leone	7, 8, 15, 16, 22, 58, 87, 98
Singapore	7, 8, 15, 16, 22, 98
Slovakia	87, 98, 130, 163, 164
Slovenia	8, 9, 16, 22, 23, 53, 56, 69, 73, 74, 87, 91, 92, 98, (109), 138
Solomon Islands	8, 16, 108
Somalia	16, 22, 23
Spain	(7), 8, 9, (15), 16, 22, 23, 53, 55, (56), (58), 68, 69, (70), 73, 74, 87, (91), 92, 98, 108, (109), 134, 138, 145, 146, 147, 163, 164, 165, 166
Sri Lanka	7, 8, 15, 16, 58, 98
Sudan	98
Suriname	87
Swaziland	87, 98
Sweden	(7), 8, 9, (15), 16, (58), 73, (75), 87, 92, 98, 108, 130, 133, 134, 138, 145, 146, 147, 163, 164
Switzerland	8, 15, 16, 23, 58, 87, 163
Syrian Arab Republic	53, 87, 98
Tanzania, United Republic of	15, 16, 98, 134
Togo	87, 98, 138
Trinidad and Tobago	15, 16, 87, 98
Tunisia	8, 16, 22, 23, 55, 58, 73, 87, 91, 98, 108
Turkey	15, 58, 98
Uganda	98
Ukraine	(15), 16, 23, (58), 69, 73, 87, 92, 98, 108, 133, 138
United Kingdom	7, 8, 15, 16, 22, 23, 56, 68, 69, (70), 74, 87, 92, 98, 108, 133, 147
United States	53, (54), 55, (57), 58, 74, 147
Uruguay	(7), 8, 9, (15), 16, 22, 23, (54), (58), 73, 87, (93), 98, 108, 130, 133, 134, 138
Venezuela	(7), 22, 87, 98, 130, 138
Yemen	15, 16, 58, 87, 98
Yugoslavia	(7), 8, 9, (15), 16, 22, 23, 53, 56, (58), 69, 73, 74, 87, 91, 92, 98, (109), 138
Zaire	98
Zambia	138

ANNEX IV

DECLARATIONS OF APPLICATION OF CONVENTIONS TO NON-METROPOLITAN TERRITORIES[1]
(as at 14 December 1993)

Member State	Non-metropolitan territory	Conventions applicable (with or without modifications)
Australia	Norfolk Islands	87, 98
Denmark	Faeroe Islands	7, 8, 9, 15, 16, 53, 87, 92, 98
Denmark	Greenland	7, 15, 16, 87
France	French Guiana	8, 9, 15, 16, 22, 23, 53, (54), 55, 56, 58, 68, 69, (70), 71, (72), 73, 74, 87, (91), 92, 98, 108, (109), 133, 145, 146, 147
France	French Polynesia	9, 15, 16, 22, 23, 53, 55, 56, 58, 69, 71, 73, 87, (91), 98, 108, 145, 146, 147
France	French Southern and Antarctic Territories	8, 9, 15, 16, 22, 23, 53, 58, 68, 69, 73, 74, 87, 92, 98, 108, 133, 134, 146, 147
France	Guadeloupe	8, 9, 15, 16, 22, 23, 53, (54), 55, 56, 58, 68, 69, (70), 71, (72), 73, 74, 87, (91), 92, 98, 108, (109), 133, 145, 146, 147
France	Martinique	8, 9, 15, 16, 22, 23, 53, (54), 55, 56, 58, 68, 69, (70), 71, (72), 73, 74, 87, (91), 92, 98, 108, (109), 133, 145, 146, 147
France	New Caledonia	9, 15, 16, 22, 23, 53, 55, 56, 58, 69, 71, 73, 87, (91), 98, 108, 145, 146, 147
France	Réunion	8, 9, 15, 16, 22, 23, 53, (54), 55, 56, 58, 68, 69, (70), 71, (72), 73, 74, 87, (91), 92, 98, 108, (109), 133, 145, 146, 147
France	St. Pierre and Miquelon	9, 15, 16, 22, 23, 53, 55, 56, 58, 69, 71, 73, 87, (91), 98, 108, 145, 146, 147
Netherlands	Aruba	8, 9, 22, 23, (58), 69, 74, 87, 138, 145, 146, 147
Netherlands	Netherlands Antilles	8, 9, 22, 23, 58, 69, 74, 87
New Zealand	Cook Islands	Nil
New Zealand	Niue	Nil
New Zealand	Tokelau	Nil
United Kingdom	Anguilla	7, 8, 22, 23, 58, 87, 98, 108
United Kingdom	Bermuda	7, 15, 16, 22, 23, 58, 87, 98, 108, 133, 147
United Kingdom	British Virgin Islands	7, 8, 23, 58, 87, 98, 108

---

[1] Numbers in parentheses denote Conventions ratified but not in force for the country concerned.

Maritime labour Conventions and Recommendations

Member State	Non-metropolitan territory	Conventions applicable (with or without modifications)
United Kingdom	Falkland Islands (Malvinas)	7, 8, 22, 23, 58, 87, 98, 108
United Kingdom	Hong Kong	7, 8, 15, 16, 22, 23, 58, 74, 87, 92, 98, 108, 133, 147
United Kingdom	Gibraltar	7, 8, 15, 16, 22, 23, 58, 87, 98, 108, 133, 147
United Kingdom	Guernsey	7, 8, 15, 16, 22, 56, 69, 74, 87, 98, 108
United Kingdom	Jersey	7, 8, 15, 16, 22, 56, 69, 74, 87, 98, 108
United Kingdom	Montserrat	7, 8, 15, 16, 58, 87, 98, 108
United Kingdom	St. Helena	7, 8, 15, 16, 58, 87, 98, 108
United Kingdom	Isle of Man	7, 8, 15, 16, 22, 23, 56, 68, 69, (70), 74, 87, 92, 98, 108, 147
United States	American Samoa	53, (54), 55, (57), 58, 147
United States	Guam	53, (54), 55, (57), 58, 74, 147
United States	Northern Mariana Islands	147
United States	Pacific Islands Trust Territory (Palau)	53, 147
United States	Puerto Rico	53, (54), 55, (57), 58, 74, 147
United States	United States Virgin Islands	53, (54), 55, (57), 58, 74, 147

INDEX